ISBN: 978-1-917731-11-9 (hardcover)
ISBN: 978-1-917731-10-2 (paperback)
ISBN: 978-1-917731-09-6 (kindle)

For enquiries regarding permissions, please contact:
Brand Story Publishing Ltd

**Disclaimer**

The views, thoughts, and opinions expressed in this book are solely those of the individual authors and do not necessarily reflect the views of Brand Story Publishing Ltd or any affiliated parties. Each author is responsible for the accuracy, authenticity, and legality of their own contributions, including any real-life experiences, personal stories, or opinions shared.

While efforts have been made to ensure that all content is presented with integrity and respect, Brand Story Publishing Ltd make no representations or warranties regarding the completeness, reliability, or accuracy of the material contained herein. Any names, locations, or identifying details are the responsibility of the individual authors.

This book is intended for informational and inspirational purposes only. It does not constitute professional, legal, medical, or psychological advice. Brand Story Publishing Ltd disclaim any liability for any errors, omissions, or consequences arising from the use or interpretation of the content. Readers should seek appropriate professional guidance where necessary.

By engaging with this book, readers acknowledge and accept that Brand Story Publishing Ltd and any affiliated parties are not responsible for any claims, disputes, or legal matters arising from the contributions of the individual authors..

# START OVER

## TURN ANY LOSS INTO A SENSATIONAL COMEBACK

# VOL 4

*14 Remarkable Authors Reveal their Powerful Journeys of Life Changing Transformation*

WITH INTERNATIONAL
NUMBER ONE BESTSELLING AUTHOR

MARCO ROBINSON

START OVER VOL 4

# Contents

INTRODUCTION

# Start Over

## *Turn Any Loss into a Sensational Comeback*

There are moments in life that tear us down so completely, we can barely see a way forward. Sometimes it's betrayal from family or friends that cuts deep, or the collapse of everything we've built – a business, a bank account, a life's work. For others, it's the quiet yet crushing trauma of abuse, or manipulation by those we trusted most.

Inside this book you'll read about men and women who hit rock bottom, faced their darkest hour and fought their way back.

The stories that follow are from those who have taken life's hardest blows. Each of them hit a point where they could have given up – and some nearly did. But instead, they chose to start over, to rise from their lowest point, and to create a life more powerful and purposeful than they had ever dreamed.

This book isn't just a collection of stories. It's a guide, a roadmap, and a call to action. The people you'll meet in these pages aren't just survivors; they're gladiators in life's arena, still battling every day to find purpose, resilience and meaning. They've transformed their trauma and pain into fuel for a sensational comeback. And through each of their stories, you'll find not only inspiration but practical steps and tools to help you take your own life from the shadows to the light.

No matter what you're facing – whether it's financial collapse, betrayal, physical trauma, abuse, or feeling trapped in a life that doesn't fulfill you – this book shows you that you can start over. You'll see how these individuals built themselves back up from the very edges of despair, harnessing their struggles to create lives of deep meaning and unshakable strength.

As you turn these pages, know that you're not alone. The warriors in this book have been there, in the depths of despair, thinking it was over. They felt the pain, the shame, the fear. And yet, they rose. They took what life threw at them and turned it into something extraordinary. Their comebacks weren't easy, but they were worth every fight, every scar, every step.

Welcome to "START OVER." This is your journey to rise, rebuild, and transform. Your comeback story starts here.

## How to Read This Book and Get the Most Out of It

This isn't just a book – it's a companion on your own journey of transformation, a guide to help you unlock the strength you may not even realize you have within you. Each chapter is a testament to the power of resilience, courage, and the relentless drive to rise again.

Here's how to make the most of every page:

1. **Read Each Story with an Open Heart and Mind:** The writers in this book have shared their most vulnerable experiences – raw, powerful stories of overcoming unimaginable challenges. These are real journeys through some of life's darkest moments: betrayal,

financial devastation, physical trauma, abuse, personal crises, and more. Each story is meant to resonate deeply, offering you insight and inspiration. As you read, allow yourself to connect to the journey, knowing that this book is here to remind you that no matter where you are, there is always a way forward.

2. **Absorb the Lessons and Insights:** At the end of each chapter, you'll find a set of lessons – hard-earned truths, perspectives, and tools that the author has gained from their experience. These lessons are the keys to starting your own comeback, allowing you to tap into the wisdom of someone who has walked through similar struggles and come out stronger. Take your time with these insights, and reflect on how they can apply to your life.

3. **Engage with the Opportunity to Connect Further:** Each writer is here not only to share their story but to offer you a bridge to connect with them directly. This isn't just a book; it's a chance to build relationships with mentors who have lived through life's greatest challenges and turned them into powerful comebacks. At the end of each chapter, you'll find a QR code. Simply scan it to connect with the author and learn more from them. This is your opportunity to ask questions, seek further guidance, and even receive resources or support tailored to help you on your own journey.

4. **Take Action on Your Own Comeback Journey:** Use each chapter as fuel to inspire your own steps forward. Whether it's a small step or a major life shift, let the stories and the lessons within them empower you

to start over, to rebuild, and to create a new path for yourself. Remember, these aren't just stories of survival; they are blueprints for transformation.

5. **Reflect and Journal Your Own Thoughts and Lessons:** As you read, keep a journal nearby. Write down any emotions, thoughts, or realizations that arise. You'll likely find that these stories unlock parts of your own life journey, bringing to light the resilience you already have within. Document your journey as you read through this book – it's a powerful tool for creating your own comeback story.

This book is here to guide you, to remind you that you are not alone, and to empower you with the wisdom of those who have faced the fire and come out transformed. Embrace each chapter, reach out to any author, and let these pages be your companion as you walk your own path toward a sensational comeback.

Your journey begins now.

START OVER VOL 4

CHAPTER

# 1

# Now I'm a Believer

MARCO ROBINSON

By 1989, the familiar walls of the clothes shop where I worked had become my prison. Three years of folding garments and making small talk with customers had taught me everything I needed to know about retail, and everything I needed to know about myself too. I was dying inside, one mundane transaction at a time.

Sure, the shop represented safety, but it also represented stagnation. My weekly wage barely covered the basics, and the prospect of ever owning a home, building a life, or creating something meaningful felt as distant as the stars. I was twenty-two years old, and I could already see the arc of my life stretching ahead: forty more years of the same conversations, the same routines, the same slow surrender to mediocrity.

But here's the thing. Sometimes, when you're trapped in your own story, the universe sends you a messenger.

Phil had been my manager at the shop before leaving for something called "direct sales." I remembered him as confident, ambitious—someone who always seemed to know where he was going. When he walked back through those familiar doors in spring 1989, everything about him had changed. There was an energy around him, a sense of possibility that made the air itself feel different.

"Marco," he said, settling into the chair across from my desk in the back office, "I want to talk to you about an opportunity."

The word hung between us like a challenge. *Opportunity?* In my world, opportunities were things that happened to other people - people with connections, education, or just better luck than mine.

"I'm working in timeshare sales now," Phil continued, his eyes bright with the kind of enthusiasm I'd forgotten existed. "We're expanding the team, and I think you'd be perfect for it."

*Timeshare sales.* The words conjured up images of smooth-talking salespeople in expensive suits, the kind of people who could convince anyone of anything. People who were everything I wasn't.

"It's commission only," Phil admitted, watching my face carefully. "But Marco, the potential is unlimited. I'm making more in a month than you make in a year here."

I felt the familiar tightness in my chest, the voice that had been my constant companion since childhood whispering its familiar refrain: *You're not good enough for that. You're not smart enough. You don't have what it takes.*

"I appreciate the offer, Phil," I said, forcing a smile. "But I'm not really a sales type, me."

He leant forward, his expression serious. "Marco, you've been here three years. Where do you see yourself in five more?"

His question hit me like a physical blow because I couldn't answer it. Five years from now, I'd be twenty-seven, still folding clothes, still living paycheque to paycheque, still wondering if this was all there was to life.

Phil visited two more times over the following weeks, each time with the same offer, the same confidence in my potential that I couldn't see myself. Each time, I found new reasons to say no. The salary was too low - just £100 a week for the first month. The location was too far - Wilmslow, near Manchester, a world away from everything familiar. The risk was too great. What if I failed?

But Phil's words kept on echoing in my mind during the long, quiet hours in the shop that folllowed: *Where do you see yourself in five more years?*

Summer turned to autumn, and the question haunted me. I'd catch myself staring out the shop window, watching people hurry past with purpose and direction, and wonder what it would feel like to be one of them. To have somewhere important to go, something meaningful to do.

The breaking point came on a particularly grey October morning. I was unpacking a delivery of winter coats—the same styles we'd sold the year before, and the year before that—when I suddenly stopped mid-motion. The coat in my hands felt impossibly heavy, as if it were made of lead instead of wool.

*This is it,* I thought. *This is my bloody life.*

The realisation was both devastating and liberating. I could stay safe, secure in my predictable routine, slowly dying inside. Or I could leap into the unknown and risk everything for the chance at something more.

That afternoon, I called Phil.

"I'll take it," I said, my voice steadier than I felt. "When do I start?"

There was a pause, then Phil's delighted laughter. "Marco, you've just made the best decision of your life."

I hoped he was right. But I was terrified he was wrong.

The journey to Wilmslow felt like travelling to another planet. As the train pulled away from everything familiar, I pressed my face to the window and watched my old life disappear behind me. The weight of what I'd done settled on my shoulders like a heavy coat.

I'd left behind not just a job, but a whole identity. For three years, I'd been "Marco from the clothes shop" - safe, predictable, unremarkable. Now I was nobody, heading towards something I didn't understand, armed with nothing but a desperate hope that I could become someone different.

The office in Wilmslow was everything Phil had promised and more. Modern, bustling with energy, filled with people who moved with purpose and spoke with confidence. The walls were covered with motivational posters and sales achievement boards, creating an atmosphere of ambition and possibility that both thrilled and terrified me.

During my first week of training, I felt like an impostor at a party I hadn't been invited to. The other trainees seemed to speak a different language—one of closing ratios and objection handling, of market penetration and customer psychology. They threw around terms like "rapport building" and "assumptive close" with the casual ease of people discussing the weather.

I sat in the back, frantically taking notes, trying to absorb concepts that felt as foreign as advanced calculus. The trainer, a sharp-suited man named David, had a way of making everything sound simple and logical. Build rapport with the customer. Identify their needs. Present the solution. Handle objections. Close the sale.

Simple, perhaps, but not easy. Not for someone like me.

"Sales," David explained on the third day, his voice carrying the authority of someone who'd closed thousands of deals, "is about belief. You have to believe in your product, believe in your company, and most importantly, believe in yourself. Without that foundation, everything else is just technique."

The word *belief* resonated in my chest like a struck bell. I believed in the product—the timeshare holidays were genuinely valuable, offering families affordable luxury holidays. I believed in the company—it was legitimate, ethical, with a track record of satisfied customers. But believe in myself?

That was a different story entirely.

My first day on the sales floor arrived with all the ceremony of an execution. The office buzzed with activity as experienced salespeople prepared for their appointments, checking their presentation materials, rehearsing their closing techniques. I sat at my assigned desk, staring at the phone that would connect me to my first prospects, feeling like a soldier about to charge into battle with a water pistol.

The system was straightforward enough. Prospects were generated through direct mail campaigns - families who'd responded to offers of free gifts in exchange for attending a 90-minute presentation. My job was to pick them up from reception, escort them to one of the presentation rooms, and spend the next hour and a half convincing them to invest £10,000 in a timeshare package.

£10,000. The number seemed impossible, surreal. I›d never had £10,000 in my life, had never even seen that much money in one place. How could I possibly convince someone else to part with such a sum?

My first appointment was the Johnsons, a middle-aged couple from Stockport. They arrived fifteen minutes late, clearly reluctant, speaking in hushed tones about wanting to "get this over with quickly." I escorted them to Presentation Room Three, my hands trembling slightly as I closed the door behind us.

For the next ninety minutes, I gave it everything I had. I followed David's training to the letter, building rapport by asking about their family, their interests, their holiday experiences. I presented the timeshare benefits with genuine enthusiasm, painting pictures of luxury holidays at a fraction of the usual cost. I handled their objections with carefully rehearsed responses.

And at the end of it all, Mr Johnson looked at me with something approaching pity.

"Son," he said, his voice gentle but firm, "you seem like a nice lad, but we're just not interested. We only came for the free gift."

They left with their complimentary weekend away voucher, and I sat alone in the presentation room, feeling the weight of failure settle on my shoulders like a lead blanket. One appointment down, and I'd already proved what I'd suspected all along - I wasn't cut out for this.

The pattern repeated itself over the following weeks with depressing consistency. The Millers from Oldham: not interested. The Patels from Manchester: not interested. The Thompsons from Warrington: not interested. Each rejection felt personal, confirmation of my inadequacy.

But perhaps the most frustrating part wasn't the rejections themselves—it was that I could see the value in what I was selling. The timeshare packages were genuinely good deals, offering families the chance to holiday in luxury resorts for a fraction of the normal cost. The company was reputable, with thousands of satisfied customers and a proven track record.

The problem wasn't the product. The problem was me.

By my sixth week, I'd achieved something of a company record - the longest streak without a sale in the office's history. Six weeks, fourteen appointments, zero sales. I could feel the sympathetic glances from my colleagues, the whispered conversations that stopped when I entered a room.

The walk home each evening became a ritual of self-torture. Five kilometres through the Manchester suburbs, my feet keeping time with the relentless rhythm of my thoughts: *Why am I such a loser? Why can't I sell? Why can't I break through?*

The questions echoed in my mind like a broken record, each repetition driving the knife of inadequacy deeper into my chest. I began to fantasise about returning to the clothes shop, about calling my old manager and begging for my job back.

At least there, I'd known what I was doing. At least there, I'd been competent.

*Maybe I should go back and clean floors again,* I thought during one particularly dark evening walk. *Maybe I should go back to the clothes shop. Maybe this whole thing was a right bloody mistake.*

But even as the thoughts formed, something deeper inside me rebelled against them. I'd tasted possibility, had felt the electricity of ambition, however briefly. Going back felt like dying.

The crisis came on a Tuesday morning in my seventh week. I was sitting at my desk, preparing for another day of inevitable rejection, when our sales manager, Tony, approached. Tony was a good man, someone who'd been rooting for me from the beginning, but the expression on his face told me everything I needed to know.

"Marco," he said, settling into the chair beside my desk, "we need to talk."

The words every failing employee dreads. I felt my stomach drop into my shoes.

"Listen, mate," Tony continued, his voice gentle but firm, "we love you to bits. Everyone here does. You're a good lad, you work hard, and you've got a great attitude. But..."

The word hung in the air like a sword of Damocles.

"But you've got to sell something. If you don't get a sale in the next couple of days, we're going to have to let you go."

Strangely, the ultimatum didn't sink in immediately. I nodded, thanked Tony for his honesty, and went through the motions of the rest of the day. It wasn't until I was walking home that evening that the full weight of his words hit me.

*If you don't get a sale in the next couple of days, we're going to have to let you go.*

I was about to lose everything. Again.

The thought of returning to my hometown, to the familiar cycle of dead-end jobs and small dreams, filled me with a panic so intense it was almost physical. I'd escaped once, had dared to reach for something better, and now I was about to fall back into the same trap that had held me prisoner for so long.

But as I walked through the darkening streets of Wilmslow, something inside me began to change. The panic was transforming into something else—a fierce, desperate determination. I wasn't ready to give up. Not yet.

That night, I couldn't sleep. I paced my small flat, the walls seeming to close in on me with each step. The question that had been my constant companion for weeks was still there, but something about it felt different now.

*Why am I such a loser?*

No. That wasn't right any more. That question had brought me nothing but pain and self-doubt. It was time for a different question.

*How can I succeed?*

The shift was subtle but profound. Instead of focusing on my failures, I was suddenly focused on possibilities. Instead of asking why I couldn't, I was asking how I could.

I walked to the window and looked out at the quiet street below. Somewhere in the distance, I could hear the sound of a train, carrying people towards their destinations, their dreams, their futures. I wanted to be on that train.

*How can I succeed?*

I said it out loud this time, my voice echoing in the small room. Then louder. Then louder still.

Before I knew it, I was walking through the streets of Wilmslow at two in the morning, asking the question to the empty air, to the sleeping houses, to the stars themselves. People would probably think I was mad, but I didn't care. Something had awakened inside me, a hunger and determination I'd never felt before.

*How can I succeed? How can I succeed? How can I succeed?*

I arrived at the office the next morning with a different energy—not confidence exactly, but something rawer and more desperate. A determination born of necessity. I was a man with nothing left to lose, and that made me dangerous.

As I settled at my desk, preparing for what might be my final day, I noticed someone approaching from across the office. It was James Mitchell, the top salesperson in the company. James was a legend—the man who consistently closed the biggest deals, who made sales look effortless, who commanded respect from everyone in the office.

He'd never spoken to me before. Why would he? I was the office failure, the guy who couldn't sell water in a desert. But now he was walking directly towards me, his expression serious.

"Marco," he said, pulling up a chair, "I heard what Tony said yesterday."

I nodded, not trusting my voice.

"I don't want you to leave," James continued. "You've got something special - something most people don't have. I can see it, even if you can't."

The words seemed impossible. James Mitchell, the top salesperson, could see something special in me?

"What do you mean?" I managed to ask.

James leant forward, his eyes intense. "I used to be like you, believe it or not. Couldn't sell anything, doubted myself constantly. I was about to quit when someone who worked here before me took me under his wing. He saw something in me that I couldn't see in myself."

The parallel was stunning. Here was this successful, confident man telling me he'd once been in exactly my position.

"That person saved my career," James continued. "He gave me some coaching, and more importantly, he gave me a book. A book that changed everything for me. And now I want to do the same for you."

He reached into his briefcase and pulled out a slim paperback. The cover was worn, obviously well-read, with the title in bold letters: "The Magic of Believing" by Claude Bristol.

"I want you to read this," James said, placing the book in my hands. "But don't just read it - study it. Absorb it. Don't stop until you get the message."

I looked down at the book, feeling its weight in my hands. It seemed too simple, too small to contain the transformation I desperately needed.

"And Marco," James added, his voice dropping to almost a whisper, "don't tell anyone you're reading it. Keep it quiet. This is between us."

The secrecy felt almost mystical, as if he were passing on ancient wisdom that could only be shared between master and apprentice.

"What's the message?" I asked.

James smiled. "You'll know when you find it." smiled. "You'll know when you find it."

That evening, I began reading "The Magic of Believing" with the intensity of a drowning man clutching a life preserver. The book's central premise was revolutionary to someone like me: that belief was the most powerful force in human achievement, that our thoughts and convictions literally shaped our reality.

Claude Bristol wrote about the power of visualisation, about the importance of unwavering faith in one's goals, about the necessity of taking complete responsibility for one's circumstances. But more than the concepts themselves, it was the examples that captivated me - story after story of ordinary people who had achieved extraordinary things simply by believing they could.

I read through the night, taking notes, underlining passages, letting the words sink into my consciousness like water into parched earth. When I finished, I immediately started again from the beginning.

Second reading. Third reading. Fourth.

With each pass through the book, new layers of meaning revealed themselves. I began to understand that my failure wasn't due to lack of skill or technique - it was due to lack of belief. In the product, yes, but more importantly, in myself.

By the fifth reading, I was highlighting entire pages. By the sixth, I was reading passages aloud, letting the words reshape my inner dialogue. By the seventh, I could feel something fundamental shifting inside me.

But it was the eighth reading that changed everything.

I was sitting in my chair at three in the morning, the book open in my lap, when suddenly the words seemed to leap off the page and embed themselves in my consciousness. It was as if I'd been looking at the book through frosted glass, and suddenly the glass had cleared.

*Belief is the most powerful force in human achievement.*

*Your thoughts become your reality.*

*You must believe in yourself before anyone else will believe in you.*

The messages weren't just intellectual concepts any more—they were living truths that I could feel in my bones. An electric energy began coursing through my body, starting in my chest and spreading outward until every cell seemed to vibrate with possibility.

I understood now why I'd been failing. Every time I'd sat across from a prospect, my inner voice had been whispering: *You're not good enough. You don't deserve success. They're going to see right through you.*

And they had. Not because I lacked skill, but because I lacked belief.

But now, for the first time in my life, I believed. I believed in the product, in the company, and most importantly, in myself. The transformation was so complete, so profound, that I could barely contain the energy building inside me.

I had to get to the office. I had to test this new version of myself.

I ran the entire five kilometres to the office, my feet pounding the pavement in rhythm with my racing heart. By the time I arrived, I was soaked in sweat, my hair plastered to my forehead, my clothes clinging to my body. The security guard took one look at me and suggested I go home to change.

"No," I said, my voice carrying a conviction I'd never heard before. "I need to be here."

The receptionist raised an eyebrow but handed me a towel. "Your first appointment is in an hour, Marco. Mr and Mrs Smith."

Mr and Mrs Smith. The names seemed almost too generic to be real, but I didn't care. I was ready for anyone, ready for anything.

An hour later, I walked to the reception area to collect my prospects. The Smiths were sitting in the corner, an elderly couple who looked distinctly uncomfortable. What struck me immediately was their guide dog, a golden retriever lying patiently at their feet.

Guide dog. The realisation hit me like a physical blow.

They were blind.

For a moment, the old Marco tried to resurface, the voice of doubt whispering: *How can you possibly sell a timeshare to people who can't see? How the hell can you show them the beautiful resorts, the luxurious accommodations, the stunning locations?*

But the new Marco, the one forged in the fire of belief, saw it differently. This wasn't an obstacle - it was a test. The universe was presenting me with the ultimate challenge: prove that belief truly was more powerful than circumstances.

"Mr and Mrs Smith?" I said, approaching their table. "I'm Marco. I'll be taking care of you today."

Mrs Smith looked up with eyes that didn't quite focus. "We'd like to leave now, please. We've changed our minds."

The old Marco would have apologised, handed them their gift voucher, and watched them walk away. But the new Marco felt something different - a calm certainty, an unshakeable faith in what was about to happen.

"I understand," I said, my voice warm and confident. "But you've come all this way, and I promise you're going to absolutely love what I have to show you. It's going to cost you £10,000, and at the end of our time together, you're going to give me your credit card."

Mr Smith looked startled. "Young man, we are definitely not interested in spending £10,000 on anything."

"That's what you think now," I replied, my smile audible in my voice. "But that's going to change. Trust me."

What happened next was something I'd never experienced before. Instead of following a script or trying to remember techniques, I simply talked to them. I told them about the product with genuine enthusiasm, painted pictures with words since they couldn't see with their eyes, shared stories of families who'd created lifetime memories through the timeshare programme.

But more than that, I listened. I asked questions about their lives, their dreams, their experiences. I learnt that they'd been married for forty-three years, that they'd always loved to travel but had been limited by their circumstances. I discovered that Mrs Smith had always dreamt of staying in a luxury resort, that Mr Smith had wanted to show his wife the world but had worried about the cost.

For five hours, I painted pictures with words, shared my absolute conviction that this product would transform their lives, and most importantly, I believed every word I said. Not because I was trying to sell them something, but because I genuinely knew it would make their lives better.

When I finally finished my presentation, the room fell silent. Mr and Mrs Smith sat holding hands, their faces reflecting deep thought. The silence stretched on for what felt like hours but was probably only minutes.

Finally, Mr Smith reached into his back pocket and pulled out his wallet. He set it on the table between us.

"Marco," he said, his voice barely above a whisper, "please find my gold credit card."

I stared at the wallet, hardly believing what I was hearing. "I'm sorry, what?"

"You were right," Mrs Smith said, tears streaming down her face. "We were wrong. This is the most amazing thing we've ever heard. We want to start using it right away."

With trembling hands, I found the gold credit card and placed it in Mr Smith's palm. He held it out to me with a smile that seemed to light up the entire room.

"Congratulations on your first sale," he said.

My first sale. The words echoed in my mind like a victory bell. I had done it. I had bloody well done it.

But more than the sale itself, what amazed me was how it had happened. I hadn't used high-pressure techniques or manipulative tactics. I had simply believed - in the product, in the value it would bring to their lives, and most importantly, in myself.

"Can I ask you something?" I said, my curiosity overcoming my professional composure. "Why did you buy from me?"

Mr Smith leant forward, his sightless eyes somehow seeming to look directly into mine. "Because you transferred your belief to us. When we felt how much you believed in this product, how much you believed it would help us, we started to believe it too."

*You transferred your belief to us.*

The words hit me like lightning. This was the secret James had been talking about, the message hidden in the book I'd read eight times. Sales wasn't about technique or manipulation—it was about belief. Pure, unshakeable belief that communicated itself from one person to another.

That £10,000 sale was just the beginning. Over the following weeks, something extraordinary happened. Armed with my new understanding of belief, I began closing deals with increasing frequency. The techniques I'd learnt in training suddenly made sense, not as manipulation tools but as ways to communicate my genuine conviction.

Within a month, I was salesperson of the month. Within six months, I was salesperson of the year. The transformation was so complete, so dramatic, that people began asking me what had changed. How had the office failure become the top performer?

The answer was simple, though not easy: I had learnt to believe.

At twenty-two years old, I was promoted to sales manager, leading a team of people who were now my age at fifty-seven. But the real transformation wasn't in my career—it was in my understanding of what was possible when someone truly believed in themselves.

I began to study the top performers in our company, and I noticed something remarkable: they all had that same quality of unshakeable belief. They didn't just think their product was good - they knew it was transformational. They didn't just hope their prospects would buy - they expected it.

And because they expected it, it happened.

The promotion brought new challenges. As sales manager, I wasn't just responsible for my own performance - I had to help others achieve theirs. When deals reached a sticking point, I'd be called to the table to help close them. To my amazement, I found I could close more deals than the entire rest of the company combined. The belief that had transformed my own sales career seemed to be transferable, something I could share with others.

My reputation grew beyond our office walls. Word spread through the industry about the young manager who could turn around any deal, who could see potential where others saw only problems. The company loved having me, but I loved the work even more. For the first time in my life, I felt like I was exactly where I belonged.

But business is unpredictable, and success can be fleeting. One day, without warning, the company made a decision that changed everything. They were closing down operations, making us all redundant. Just like that, my newfound career seemed to be over.

Yet something interesting happened. Instead of panic, I felt... calm. The old Marco would have been devastated, would have seen this as confirmation of his unworthiness. But the new Marco understood something different: I hadn't just learned to sell timeshares. I had learned to believe in myself, and that was transferable to any situation.

The company still had offices in Tenerife, but they were planning to close those too. Most people would have seen this as the end of the road, but I saw it as an opportunity. I had made a name for myself, had proven what was possible when someone truly believed in their abilities.

I made a decision that would have seemed impossible to the old Marco. I drove to see the top boss, the man who had the power to keep the Tenerife operation running. I wasn't going to beg for a job - I was going to offer him a solution.

"Listen," I said, sitting across from him in his office, "I know you're planning to close Tenerife. But what if I told you I could turn it into your most profitable operation? What if I could recruit and train a team that would generate more sales than all your other offices combined?"

He looked at me for a long moment, probably wondering if this young man was completely mad. But there was something in my voice, something in my conviction, that made him listen.

"You're persistent, I'll give you that," he said finally. "How many times have you come to see me about this?"

"As many times as it takes," I replied. "Because I believe in what I can do for you, me."

There it was again. Belief. The foundation of everything.

He leant back in his chair, a smile playing at the corners of his mouth. "Alright, Marco. I admire your conviction. Let's try it. Come to Tenerife. We'll make you the recruitment and training manager. Show me what you can do."

And so began the next chapter of my journey. I moved to Tenerife, where I recruited and trained salespeople using the same principles that had transformed my own career. I taught them about belief, about the power of conviction, about the magic that happens when you truly know your product can change people's lives.

The results were extraordinary. Our team became the best in the company, generating more sales than operations twice our size. I had proven that the principles I'd learned weren't just personal - they were universal. Anyone could learn to believe, and anyone who truly believed could achieve remarkable things.

But success, as I was learning, often attracts change. The company was eventually sold, and once again, I found myself without a job. Yet once again, I felt that same calm confidence. I had something now that no one could take away from me: the unshakeable knowledge that I could succeed at anything I set my mind to.

The offers came from all over the world. Companies who had heard about what we'd accomplished in Tenerife wanted to replicate our success. My business partner and I found ourselves in the enviable position of being able to choose our next adventure.

The best offer came from Malaysia, from a company called Tanko Resorts. They owned about thirty hotels and were a successful property development company, publicly traded and doing very well. What they wanted was to start a timeshare division, to sell hotel memberships using exactly the expertise we'd developed.

In 1997, I made a decision that would have been unthinkable to the Marco who had once folded clothes and wondered if he'd ever amount to anything. I sold everything I had - literally everything - and moved to Malaysia with my six-month-old daughter and my partner.

I remember standing in Heathrow Airport with eleven trolleys of belongings, about to board a plane to a country I'd never visited, to start a business in a culture I didn't understand. The old Marco would have been scared shitless. The new Marco saw it as the greatest adventure of his life.

We missed our first flight because of excess baggage charges, but we made the morning flight when the scales broke and we got lucky. As the plane lifted off, carrying us towards our new life, I reflected on the journey that had brought me here.

From the clothes shop to Malaysia, from self-doubt to self-belief, from asking "Why am I such a loser?" to asking "How can I succeed?" The transformation had been complete, but it had all started with a single realisation: belief is the most powerful force in human achievement.

I had learned that we all have magic within us. The question isn't whether we're capable of extraordinary things - we all are. The question is whether we believe it. And once you truly believe, once you let that belief permeate every cell of your being, everything becomes possible.

The blind couple who had bought my first timeshare had taught me that belief is transferable. James Mitchell had shown me that success leaves clues. Claude Bristol's book had given me the framework to understand it all. But the real teacher had been experience itself—the daily practice of choosing belief over doubt, possibility over limitation, growth over stagnation.

As I settled into my seat for the long flight to Malaysia, I thought about the young man I'd been just a few years earlier. That scared, uncertain person felt like a different lifetime, almost a different person entirely. Yet in another sense, he was still with me—not as a source of shame, but as a reminder of how far belief could take someone.

I had become the believer. And in becoming the believer, I had discovered that the only limits we face are the ones we accept. The only failures we experience are the ones we choose to make permanent. The only dreams that remain unfulfilled are the ones we stop believing in.

The plane banked towards the east, carrying me towards my next chapter, my next opportunity to prove that belief truly was the magic that could transform any life, any situation, any dream into reality.

## ABOUT THE AUTHOR

# MARCO ROBINSON

*Marco Robinson is an international #1 bestselling author, award-winning entrepreneur, and Top #2 Netflix producer. Renowned for creating and hosting Channel 4's prime-time TV show "Get a House for Free", where he gave homes to homeless families, Marco is a philanthropist knighted in the Commonwealth for his extraordinary charity work. A three-time winner of the prestigious Two Comma Club Award for generating millions in sales, Marco has built his legacy by inspiring people worldwide to turn loss into a sensational comeback. As the visionary behind the Start Over book series, he proves that no setback is too great to overcome.*

# CHAPTER 2

## Small But Mighty

*Invisible to Invincible*

ARLENE BARCLAY

The first time I fought back, truly fought back, I was pinned beneath a man nearly three times my size, his breath hot on my face as he growled, "Don't fight it." But fighting—surviving—is what I had been preparing for my entire life. What he didn't know as he looked down at my five-foot-two frame was that I had been forged in the fires of adversity since childhood. I may have appeared small, but inside me burned the spirit of a warrior. This is the story of how I discovered my might.

In the shadowed corners of my childhood home, I often stood alone—a solitary figure watching life unfold around me. The cacophony of my parents' two businesses created a constant backdrop to our family life, drowning out connections that might have formed between me, my older sister, and younger brother. While they moved through the house like familiar strangers, I learned early to find my own path through the darkness, my footsteps echoing in empty hallways as my parents' attention was pulled in a thousand different directions. I became accustomed to the weight of invisibility pressing against my small shoulders—never knowing this very weight would one day transform into the strength that would save my life.

At fifteen, the shadows that had followed me since childhood finally consumed me entirely. In that moment of deepest darkness, standing at the precipice between life and death, I heard the faintest whisper of my own voice—a voice I barely recognised. "Fight," it said. "You were made for more than this." That whisper, that fragile thread of hope, became my lifeline. As I pulled myself back from the edge, two guiding lights appeared in the void: fitness and faith. My body, which I had nearly destroyed, would become my temple; my spirit, nearly extinguished, would become my compass. I made a solemn vow that echoes within me still: I would never again surrender to the darkness. I would rise, stronger than before, and embrace life with everything I had.

At eighteen, I stepped across the threshold of my childhood home into a world vast with possibility. As Welfare Secretary on a North East oil rig, I found rhythm in the two-week rotations—fourteen days of purpose followed by fourteen days of reflection. The steady pulse of work and rest became the heartbeat of my new life, each cycle strengthening my newfound independence.

By twenty, that rhythm quickened as I donned the crisp uniform of a KLM air hostess. The earth fell away beneath me as I soared through clouds, each new horizon expanding my understanding of how small—yet significant—my place in the world truly was. With each takeoff and landing, I felt the gravitational pull of my past weakening, replaced by the exhilarating weightlessness of freedom.

When love found me at twenty, it arrived wearing a disguise I wouldn't recognise for years to come. His smile felt like home, his arms like sanctuary, and when our two beautiful children came into the world, I believed I had finally found the family connection I had craved since childhood.

But beneath the surface of our shared life, toxicity seeped in like rising floodwater—sometimes receding enough to let me breathe, sometimes threatening to drown me. For twenty-three years, I waded through this treacherous emotional landscape, the weight of unfulfilled promises and unspoken pain growing heavier with each passing year.

It was in the gym—surrounded by the metallic clang of weights and the rhythm of my own determined breath—that I discovered a truth my body had always known: I was stronger than I appeared. Each rep, each bead of sweat, each moment of physical challenge became a meditation on resilience. The barbell didn't care about my past; it only responded to my present strength and determination. In this raw, honest space, I began to rebuild myself from the inside out, muscle by hard-earned muscle.

In the year 2000, I embraced my calling as a fitness instructor. The role resonated deeply within me, as if every cell in my body had been waiting for this purpose. Over three transformative years, I earned personal training qualifications and various fitness certifications, each one expanding my ability to uplift others. I became not just a trainer but a motivator—someone who could guide others through their own challenges and inspire them to discover their inner strength.

My classes flourished, consistently filled to capacity with waiting lists that validated the energy and passion I poured into every session. Each packed room became testimony to the power of authentic connection—the kind I had yearned for throughout my childhood. In the rhythmic movement of bodies working in unison, I found a form of belonging I had never before experienced.

The afternoon light filtered through my kitchen windows, casting long shadows across the freshly organised consultation papers. Everything was perfect—my home transformed into a professional sanctuary, my dream of an independent personal training business finally realised. The pride swelling in my chest felt unfamiliar but welcome.

When the buzzer rang, announcing my boxing mentor's arrival, my heart quickened with anticipation. "Just come up," I called, listening to his heavy footsteps on the stairs. Each step echoed with the trust and respect we'd built through countless training sessions.

He filled the doorframe when I opened it—his six-foot frame and eighteen-stone physique commanding the space in a way that had never before made me uneasy. But something in his eyes shifted as I closed the door behind us, something predatory flickering in their depths.

"You look great," he said, his voice hanging in the air between us like smoke. The compliment landed wrong, devoid of the professional respect that had defined our relationship. A cold whisper of warning crawled up my spine, but I pushed it aside. He was a family man, well into his fifties, with a wife and grown children. This was my mentor, my client—surely I was misreading the situation.

I gestured toward the kitchen table with forced brightness. "Let's go through the paperwork before we—"

The world compressed into a single, terrifying moment. His massive body crashed against mine, the impact driving my small frame backward until the cold glass of my table pressed against my back. His breath came hot and heavy against my face, his weight pinning me down as panic exploded in my chest.

"Don't fight it," he growled, the words searing themselves into my memory.

But something primal roared to life within me. "NOOOOO!" The scream tore from my throat as a voice inside my head commanded: FIGHT IT. In that crystalline moment of terror, a truth solidified within me—I would not be broken by this man. I would not be another statistic, another victim, another woman silenced by fear.

Despite my five-foot-two frame, years of training surged through my muscles. "I may be small, but I'm mighty," the mantra flashed through my mind as I pulled my legs up beneath his weight, finding leverage against the glass table. With explosive power born from fear and fury, I drove both feet into his stomach, sending him flying backward into the kitchen cabinets with a satisfying crash.

The shock in his eyes fed something fierce within me—the realisation that he had gravely underestimated the woman he'd attempted to overpower. I became a hurricane of calculated rage, each punch and kick a declaration of my right to safety, my right to power, my right to exist without fear.

As he limped away, defeated and diminished, I slammed the door and slid to the floor, my body trembling with adrenaline and aftermath. Curled into myself, I released a sound from the deepest part of my being—raw and wounded at first, then transforming into something else entirely. I had beaten the Beast. Not just the man who had attacked me, but the fear that had shadowed me since childhood, the doubt that had whispered I wasn't strong enough to survive this world.

In that moment of both vulnerability and victory, fitness was no longer just my passion—it had become my salvation.

The woman who rose from that kitchen floor was not the same one who had opened the door an hour earlier. I carried the physical victory with me, but more importantly, I carried a profound understanding of why fitness had always called to me so strongly—it had been preparing me, strengthening me, for moments when I would need to fight for myself.

I made a solemn vow that day: I would never train a man in my home again. This boundary became the first of many I would establish in the years to come, each one a brick in the foundation of my rebuilt life. My attacker's absence from the gym became a question for others, but for me, it was a silent victory banner waving over the battlefield of my survival.

Sexual assault leaves invisible scars that no amount of physical training can erase, but I refused to let trauma become my identity. Instead, I channelled that experience into fierce determination. Each day became an opportunity to reclaim some piece of myself that had been threatened—my security, my confidence, my joy. I understood with startling clarity that no one could take my power unless I surrendered it willingly.

Fitness became more than exercise; it transformed into a moving meditation on resilience. With each rep, each mile, each drop of sweat, I was building not just a stronger body but an unbreakable spirit. The woman staring back at me in the gym mirror was becoming someone I deeply respected—someone who had been knocked down but refused to stay there, someone who transformed pain into purpose.

Seven years passed in relative peace, my days brightened by my vibrant four-year-old son whose laughter filled our home with joy. These were, perhaps, the happiest days I'd known—moments of ordinary magic that reminded me why fighting to survive had been worth every struggle.

When the news came that my beloved granny had been diagnosed with bowel cancer with only a year to live, grief wrapped its heavy arms around me. She had been my first female idol, a beacon of kindness in my tumultuous childhood, and the thought of losing her tore at my heart. I devoted myself to making her final months gentle—accompanying her to hospital appointments, dressing her with tender care, and taking her on car rides where Daniel O'Donnell's music would fill the space between us as we sang along, creating memories I would cherish forever.

In a cruel twist of fate, just as my granny entered her final weeks, I silently endured my own loss—a miscarriage the day before, my third lost pregnancy. I carried this private grief alone, unwilling to burden others with hopes that had been crushed too many times before.

Walking into her care home that day, I moved down the familiar corridor toward her flat, my heart heavy with unspoken sorrow. When my grandfather emerged to greet me, I lifted my arms for our usual embrace, a small comfort in difficult times.

"Hi Grandad," I said, summoning a smile despite my exhaustion.

The violation came without warning—his hands grabbing me inappropriately, transforming familial affection into something sinister and wrong. As he retreated into his flat as though nothing had happened, I stood frozen in the corridor, arms still lifted in expectation of an embrace that had become a betrayal.

"Did this just happen?" The question echoed in my mind, followed immediately by the answer: "Yes, it did."

In that moment, I faced a choice that would define me—confront him and create chaos during my grandmother's final days, or carry the burden silently to protect her peace. The strength I had built over years of overcoming hardship steadied me as I chose the latter, refusing to let his toxic actions poison her remaining time.

With a composure that surprised even me, I entered their flat and greeted my granny with genuine warmth. "We're going for a ladies' day out, just you and me, Granny," I announced, my voice betraying none of the turmoil beneath.

Her reply was a balm to my wounded spirit: "Oh lass, you are so good to me." I smiled back, knowing I was simply returning a fraction of the love she had always given so freely.

Three weeks later, after laying my granny to rest, I found the courage to speak my truth. I shared the assault with my family, expecting support but finding instead a wall of disbelief. "Liar," they called me, their rejection swift and absolute. I was banned from family gatherings and even my grandfather's funeral, cast out for daring to protect future generations from similar harm.

The family that had once defined me was gone, but in their absence, I discovered something remarkable—I was enough on my own. I had spoken out not for vengeance but for the safety of others, and in that knowledge, I found a peace that transcended their rejection. My job was done, and I would carry forward, guided by the love and lessons of my granny, a woman whose strength lived on in me.

To be sexually assaulted once was devastating; to endure it again at the hands of a family member was a unique kind of horror. The twin betrayals could have crushed me entirely, but I made a conscious decision: these experiences would become stepping stones, not stumbling blocks.

I threw myself into CrossFit with a fervour that surprised even me. Each workout became a battlefield where I confronted not just physical limitations but the emotional barriers I'd built around myself. The community embraced me—this woman with fire in her eyes and determination in every movement.

My physical transformation mirrored the internal one—muscles developing definition, endurance building with each gruelling workout. I cut my long red hair into a bleached blonde mohawk, an external declaration of the warrior I had become. Looking in the mirror, I barely recognised myself, but for the first time, I truly saw myself—strong, resilient, unapologetic.

They called me "Pocket Rocket" in the gym, a nickname that acknowledged both my smaller stature and the explosive power I carried within. When I qualified for Tribal Clash, competing alongside world-class athletes in a two-day event, it felt like more than an athletic achievement—it was validation that I had transcended my past.

Standing on those competition grounds, muscles burning with exertion, sweat mingling with sea spray, I realised I had built more than a strong body. I had crafted a fortress around my spirit, a place where the ghosts of past trauma could no longer reach me. I was no longer defined by what had been done to me, but by what I had done for myself.

CrossFit had built my strength, but something inside me hungered for a new challenge—one that would require mental discipline as rigorous as the physical demands. Bodybuilding called to me with its promise of complete transformation, of sculpting not just muscle but an entirely new version of myself.

I immersed myself in this world of precise nutrition, carefully planned workouts, and meticulous attention to every aspect of physical development. The discipline required touched something deep within me—a reminder that I held complete control over my body and its capabilities. Each meal prepared, each weight lifted, each pose practised became an act of reclamation.

Standing before the mirror practising poses, I saw the culmination of my journey reflected back at me—a woman who had transformed tragedy into triumph, weakness into strength, victimhood into victory. My body told a story of resilience, each defined muscle a paragraph in the narrative of my survival.

With just three weeks before my first competition, the foundation I thought was stable crumbled beneath me.

My partner of twenty-three years dropped his bombshell: he wanted "different experiences" in our relationship. The timing felt deliberately cruel, the emotional impact devastating. This relationship—the one constant through all my transformations—was ending just as I prepared to step onto the stage and show the world who I had become.

The old me might have collapsed under this new weight, might have abandoned the competition to nurse my wounded heart. But the woman I had become—the one who had faced down attackers and family rejection—knew better. I drew upon every tool I had developed throughout my journey, channelling my pain into my preparation.

When competition day arrived, I stepped onto that stage not as a victim of circumstance but as the architect of my own destiny. The lights were blinding, the audience a blur, but my presence was undeniable. Fourth place overall in my first competition wasn't just a placement—it was proof that I could face any storm and emerge not just intact but triumphant.

Leaving a toxic relationship after twenty-three years requires a special kind of courage—the kind I had been building through every challenge life had thrown at me. With clear vision and unwavering resolve, I relocated to a new town with my children, a fresh start in a place untainted by painful memories.

Balancing my roles as manager, fitness instructor, and personal trainer while parenting alone tested my limits daily. But the strength I had cultivated through years of adversity served me well. My children thrived in their new environment, and watching them bloom in this healthier atmosphere became my greatest reward.

Eight years into this new life, an opportunity that seemed like destiny appeared on my horizon—a position in Dubai running a gym, complete with an apartment and tax-free income. It felt like the universe acknowledging my hard work, offering a chance to finally leave the shadows of my past behind completely.

For nine months, I navigated a labyrinth of preparations—visa applications, passport renewals, medical exams, school arrangements for my daughter, and vaccinations for our beloved dog. I dismantled our life piece by piece, selling possessions saturated with memories, each item released with both sadness and hope.

When the devastating truth emerged—that the entire Dubai opportunity was an elaborate scam—the ground seemed to disappear beneath my feet. In one cruel moment, I found myself homeless, savings depleted, dreams shattered. The humiliation burned almost as fiercely as the fear; we had just attended our own leaving party, publicly declaring a future that had evaporated into thin air.

The only choice I had was to put my children up with my ex and our family fractured in ways I hadn't anticipated. As I returned to my parents' home, the homeless federation's estimation of a year-long wait for housing felt like a prison sentence.

In this darkest moment, when I could have surrendered to despair, I instead reclaimed the fighting spirit that had saved me so many times before. I pounded pavements daily, networking, calling every rental sign, refusing to accept that our displacement would be prolonged.

When offered a mould-infested home by the homeless federation, I made the bold choice to refuse—even knowing it meant removal from their housing list. Some might have called it foolish, but I recognised it as the same instinct that had helped me survive every previous trial: the unwavering belief that I deserved better.

The universe responds to perseverance. One ordinary day at the swimming pool—another sanctuary where I maintained my physical and mental strength—a casual conversation in the sauna led to an unexpected blessing. A stranger, overhearing my story, mentioned a two-bedroom apartment available in town. Within days, I was in contact with the landlord, and within a week—moving into apartment 13 on Friday the 13th of October. The poetry of those numbers wasn't lost on me; what others might see as unlucky, I recognised as my perfect alignment.

Just when stability seemed within reach, my body betrayed me with vertigo so severe that my twelve-year-old daughter had to call emergency services as I lost my balance, vision blurring into incomprehensible shapes. The diagnosis carried uncertainty—three days, three weeks, or three years of symptoms—but I refused to surrender to this new challenge.

In the stillness forced upon me by my condition, a moment of clarity arrived like a lightning strike. Drawing on my experience as a bodybuilder and fitness professional, I envisioned a tool that would allow me to maintain strength even with my limitations. The BOOMBAR was born from necessity—a versatile strength training tool usable from bedside, chair, or standing position.

This creation, conceived in my moment of greatest physical weakness, became my greatest strength. As it accelerated my recovery, I recognised its potential to help others rebuild themselves as I had done so many times. The BOOMBAR became more than equipment; it became a symbol of adaptation, of finding power when circumstances seem most limiting.

Throughout these nine years of healing, everything I've accomplished has formed part of a sacred journey to wholeness—mind, body, spirit aligned through experiences ranging from fire walking to open water swimming, from women's circles to deep meditation practices. These diverse paths taught me the art of presence, the power of self-love, and the importance of connecting with something greater than myself.

Every three months, I meet with my spiritual mentor for transformative sessions that ground and inspire me. These meetings remind me that being truly seen and heard is perhaps the greatest gift we can receive—and give. This supportive relationship elevates my unique vibration, keeping me connected to purpose even when life's currents grow turbulent.

My journey from invisible child to resilient woman, from assault survivor to empowered creator, from homelessness to haven-builder, has taught me that we are never defined by what happens to us, but by how we respond to life's greatest challenges. I may be small in stature, but I am mighty in spirit—a truth I carry into each new day, each new challenge, each opportunity to help others discover their own innate strength.

Today, as I guide others on their fitness journeys with the BOOMBAR, I see reflections of my own story in their eyes—the doubt, the determination, the discovery of inner strength. I recognise the warrior spirit awakening within them, just as it awakened in me. If my journey from darkness to light resonates with you, if you too are fighting to reclaim your power, remember this: your struggles don't define you—they refine you. And no matter your size, circumstances, or past, you contain within you a might that is waiting to be unleashed.

## ABOUT THE AUTHOR

# ARLENE BARCLAY

SCAN TO KNOW MORE

*Arlene Barclay is a devoted mother of two children and her cherished dog, Winter. Her journey has been marked by sheer determination and grit, fuelled by her passion for fitness and unwavering faith. Arlene is the innovative creator of the BOOMBAR, a functional strength training tool that played a crucial role in her recovery from vertigo, showcasing her commitment to health and wellness. With over 35 years of experience as a fitness instructor, she inspires others to embrace their strength and resilience. Arlene's mission is to uplift those around her, helping them navigate their own challenges and achieve their personal best.*

CHAPTER

# 3

# From Broken to Unbreakable

## *A Journey of Resilience and Redemption*

TONY HARESIGN

The brass key slid into the lock with a satisfying click as early morning light spilt across the polished floor of my barbershop. I paused, inhaling the familiar blend of sandalwood aftershave, lemon disinfectant, and that unmistakable scent of professional pride; my signature. Seven years of relentless work had transformed this space from an empty storefront to a thriving community fixture that was always booked solid for weeks into the future.

Once inside, my fingers traced the polished wooden units as I fired up the espresso machine. Steam hissed and the rich aroma of freshly ground beans filled the room. This quiet ritual - these precious moments before clients arrived, centred me for the day ahead and I relished them.

My phone vibrated. The email I'd been waiting for: confirmation that I'd be presenting my new men's hair collection at Salon International in London. My heart pounded as I took the first sip of espresso, its bitterness matching the sweet anticipation of my biggest professional opportunity yet.

Running my own business demanded everything from me, every ounce of energy, every moment of focus. But the rewards made it worthwhile. Not just the financial success, but the connections I built with my clients. Men who trusted me with more than their hair. They entrusted me with their stories, their fears, their triumphs. From ridiculous stag party escapades to intimate confessions about failing marriages, these moments of authentic connection were the true measure of my success.

Jacob, a 19-year-old surfer and triathlete, was my last client of the day. Our conversation flowed from wave technique to sports physiology, his eyes bright with the same boundless ambition that had once defined my younger self. As I sculpted his hair with practised precision, I recognised in him my own gung-ho attitude ; that beautiful belief that no challenge was too great.

"When's the tournament?" Katie asked as she prepared to lock up, sweeping hair from the gleaming floor with practised strokes.

"Two weeks," I replied, mustering confidence while my stomach knotted with the uncertainty. "Not sure if I'm ready, but I'm going to give it everything."

Hours later, the dojo's polished floor stuck against my bare feet as sweat pooled beneath me. The rhythmic slap of fists against pads created a percussion that matched my thundering heartbeat. My lungs burned with each gasping breath as we drilled our moves.

For me, it was the roundhouse kick, a devastating rotation that channelled every ounce of power from the ground up through my hips, snapping my leg like a whip against the target. The impact reverberated up my spine, a satisfying confirmation of power properly delivered.

At 49, facing opponents potentially half my age with black belts that represented decades of dedication, I pushed beyond exhaustion. My muscles screamed in protest as I executed one more kick, then another, then ten more. The metallic taste of determination filled my mouth.

This was our final intense training session before tapering down for the tournament. Though I'd practised various martial arts since age 10, this particular style was new to me. The white belt around my waist felt foreign compared to the belts I'd earned in other disciplines, yet the challenge excited me in the same way my mountain bike races across Scotland once had.

Time played its usual trick as the tournament approached stretching endlessly at first, then suddenly compressing until the day arrived without warning. The 90-minute drive to the venue seemed interminable, my stomach churning with each mile. I checked my kit repeatedly: GI, pads, gumshield, energy drinks, headphones. The familiar pre-competition jitters coursed through me ; not fear, but that electric anticipation that made me feel truly alive.

At the venue, my coach disappeared to find the day's schedule while I surveyed the scene. Competitors of all ages warmed up in designated areas, their movements precise and focused. In the main hall, spectators lined the mats where judges sat ready with their red and white flags.

"You're up at 3 p.m.," my coach announced upon his return.

"Six hours? You're kidding. I'll burn through all my adrenaline by then!" I protested.

"Just focus," he replied firmly.

Finding a quiet corner, I plugged in my headphones. David Goggins' voice filled my ears as I listened to "Can't Hurt Me," his words penetrating my consciousness, reinforcing my mental armour for the challenge ahead.

When the time finally came, my coach pulled me aside during warm-up. "Your first opponent is a 3rd Dan black belt," he said, his expression serious.

My heart sank. "Are you serious? This guy's got more experience than I've had hot dinners!" Self-doubt crept in, threatening the confidence I'd built.

"You'll be fine. Stick to the plan; quick punches to set up the roundhouse."

The referee gave us the two-minute warning. My coach's final words hung in the air: "Stick to the fucking plan!"

The tournament hall echoed with shouts and the sharp slap of bodies hitting mats. My opponent's foot connected with my head—a flash of white-hot pain, followed by the copper tang of blood filling my mouth. The ref stepped in, deducting a point, but the message was clear: this was no ordinary match.

"Right, you fucker," I thought, tasting my own blood as determination surged through me.

I launched a furious counterattack, forcing my opponent off the mat multiple times. But with fifteen seconds left and down by one point, I heard my coach through the wall of noise: "Roundhouse! Now!"

Time slowed. I pivoted on my supporting leg, chambering my right knee, and unleashed the kick I'd drilled a thousand times.

Then—a sound. Not the expected thud of connection, but something else. Something was wrong. A sickening pop that seemed to echo inside my skull before anyone else heard it.

White-hot agony exploded through my knee like a shotgun blast. The world tilted and blurred as gravity claimed me. My body collapsed onto the mat, but it was more than just my leg that broke, something fundamental inside me shattered in that same instant.

I lay there, the cold mat against my cheek, the overhead lights suddenly too bright, too harsh. The crowd's murmurs became a distant roar as though I was underwater. In those few heartbeats, I already knew, everything had changed.

The referee halted the bout. The medic rushed over, her face revealing what I already felt: this was bad. With only four seconds left on the clock, I nodded when she asked if I could continue, my pride overriding my pain.

The bout restarted, but my opponent didn't attack. He saw what I couldn't admit, I was finished. The judges raised their flags in his favour as time expired. He nodded at me, respect or pity, I couldn't tell which.

With my coach's help, I hobbled off the mat. The medic returned with a plastic bag filled with Slushie.

"Sorry, we're out of proper ice packs," a surreal detail that would have been funny in any other circumstance.

The car ride home was a symphony of pain as the makeshift ice pack melted against my swelling knee. I limped into the house, downplaying the injury to my wife, and collapsed into bed. As I lay there, watching my knee swell to grotesque proportions, a sinking feeling washed over me, it wasn't just my knee that was broken; something inside me felt shattered beyond repair.

Morning light filtered through the blinds, unwelcome and accusatory. Another day  stretched before me. I peeled back the covers, dreading what I'd see.

My leg, once strong and capable, now a grotesque stranger. My knee bulged to three times its normal size, the skin taut and shiny. Yellow streaks crawled up my calf like toxic fingers while my foot had become a canvas of purple and black. The sight alone made my stomach lurch.

"Tasha!" My voice cracked, betraying the panic I was trying to contain.

Her sharp intake of breath when she entered told me everything I needed to know. This wasn't normal. This wasn't getting better.

By the time we reached Stuart, a former physio for the Scottish rugby team, even he couldn't mask his horror. He called in two colleagues, their whispered, grave observations intensifying my already desperate frame of mind.

"You need to go straight to the hospital... Now!"

The hospital visit ended with painkillers, a full leg brace, and instructions to wait for an MRI. The specialist's words rang in my ears long after he spoke them: "This will need an operation and take 12 to 18 months, maybe longer to recover. You'll need relentless physio. It's going to be hard."

Hard wasn't the word for it.

Days blurred into weeks. Pain became my constant companion and not just the physical agony that radiated from my knee with each heartbeat, but a deeper ache that settled in my chest. As a man who had always defined himself through physical prowess and providing for his family, each assisted trip to the bathroom felt like another piece of my identity being stripped away.

For over a week, I was confined to my bed, dependent on my wife and children for the most basic needs. The indignity crushed what remained of my self-image. I had never felt so distant from myself, as if the person I had been ; confident, strong, unstoppable, was slipping away, replaced by a shell I didn't recognise.

Depression seeped into the cracks of my psyche like a slow, insidious poison. I tried to mask it, even from myself, but the signs were unmistakable: smoking too much weed, retreating from family conversations, lying in bed for hours staring at the ceiling, feeling nothing and everything all at once.

Sixteen months later, with COVID shutting down my business and cancelling nine shows in four days, I hit rock bottom. The financial collapse mirrored my physical state, broken, useless, a shell of what I once was. For a week, I barely left the bed, the sheets becoming a shroud, the darkness a companion.

The thought crept into my mind, unwelcome, terrifying, but persistent: perhaps the world would be better off without me. Maybe my family would find peace without this broken version of me dragging them down, and I would be free from this torment. The idea scared me, but in the darkest hours, when pain kept sleep at bay, it visited with increasing frequency.

Then, on a grey afternoon when nothing felt different, I clipped the leash on our dog and hobbled toward the coastal path. The wind carried the sharp tang of salt and seaweed. Gulls wheeled overhead, their cries somehow both mournful and free.

Something stirred within me. A memory of who I used to be.

Without planning, without thinking, I picked up my pace. It was awkward, painful, nothing like my former running form, but at least I was moving. The wind rushed past my ears. My heart pounded. My damaged knee protested with each impact, but beneath the pain, something else emerged.

Life. I was alive.

That night, I found myself scrolling through Instagram, and a post stopped my thumb. Ben Turner, The Adventure Coach. His words about resilience and rebirth seemed written directly to me, as though he could see through the screen to the broken man on the other side.

My fingers hovered over the keyboard. Reaching out felt like admitting defeat, yet also like the first genuine step forward in over a year. I sent a message into the void, not knowing if it would return with hope or silence.

After long conversations with Ben and deep soul-searching, we crafted a plan. The first goal was modest but meaningful:

a half marathon. As the fog of depression began to lift with each training run, I set my sights on something greater; a full marathon to raise money for suicide prevention.

The catalyst for that decision arrived with devastating clarity. "Mate," a friend said one December evening, his voice choked with emotion, "He's gone... he took his own life."

I couldn't breathe. The friend he referred to had been confident and charismatic, the kind of person who could walk into a room and lift everyone's spirits. The idea that someone like him could be suffering in silence broke me. The pain was raw and deep, leaving an empty feeling in my stomach.

But it also ignited a fire within me. I needed to do something. For him. For the countless men struggling under the weight of their own darkness. For myself.

The marathon became more than a physical challenge—it became a symbol of hope, a way to channel my grief into something meaningful. While training along coastal paths and through muddy forests, I thought of him. Of the men who would never speak up, who carried their burdens alone until it became too much. Suicide is the biggest killer of men under 40 in the UK; a statistic that haunted me with each step.

I wasn't alone in my mission. Jacob, the young triathlete client who had reminded me so much of my younger self, joined me in training. He too had lost a friend to suicide—at just 21 years old—a stark reminder that this darkness touched men of all ages.

The marathon course circled Loch Leven, a 13-mile loop we would run twice. With COVID restrictions still in place, there were no organised events, no cheering crowds—just Jacob and me against the distance and our own demons.

Each step around the loch carried meaning beyond the physical journey. Together, we raised over £3,000 for Samaritans—enough to fund hundreds of calls offering support to those in desperate need.

As I crossed the finish line, legs trembling and lungs burning, I felt something I hadn't experienced in nearly two years: purpose. The marathon hadn't just tested my physical endurance; it had proven that my broken pieces could still form something whole, something meaningful.

But it wasn't enough. The ache in my chest told me there was still more to do.

I would run the ten highest mountains in the UK in just 4 days..

For seven months, I threw myself into gruelling training, coached by Ben. Each step up a hill or mountain became a testament to the resilience I was rediscovering within myself. I ran through snow, rain, fog, and darkness—up mountains and through forests, across muddy paths and rocky terrain—to prepare my body and mind for the ultimate test.

In May, it was time.

The adventure began on the rugged slopes of Ben Lawers. Familiar terrain greeted me, but the snowline at 600 meters transformed it into a punishing trial. I pushed through the biting cold and icy winds, the summit feeling more like a battleground than a victory. And this was only the beginning.

Day two was monstrous—five peaks in the Cairngorms, including Cairn Gorm, Ben Macdui, Angel's Peak, Cairn Toul, and the mighty Braeriach. The relentless climbs, knee-deep snow, and near white-out conditions tested me in ways I never anticipated. My legs burned, my lungs screamed for air, and my resolve wavered with every step. By the end of the 33-kilometre loop, I was shattered.

My feet were blistered and bloodied, one toenail barely hanging on. I stuffed as much food as I could manage into my body, taped the toenail back in place, and collapsed into exhausted sleep.

Day three brought new challenges in the Nevis range, where the mist was so thick I had to rely on compass bearings to avoid veering off treacherous ridges. The isolation was profound—no encouraging words from fellow hikers, no visible path ahead, just me and the mountain and my will to keep moving forward.

Day four dawned with Càrn Mòr Dearg. A mountain lying in the shadow of Ben Nevis. My torn toenail hung by a thread, taped in place like my fragile resolve and every muscle fibre screamed for relief. The plan was ambitious: ascend Càrn Mòr Dearg, traverse the narrow ridge known as the Càrn Mòr Dearg Arête, and then scale Ben Nevis via its daunting north face.

But Mother Nature had other plans. By the time I reached the top of Càrn Mòr Dearg, the wind howled at over 60 miles per hour. The gusts were relentless, forcing me to reconsider crossing the exposed and treacherous ridge.

The same wind that tried to dislodge me from the mountain carried away my doubt. With each step, I shed another layer of the man I was after the injury, the man who believed he was finished, who contemplated an end to his pain.

I thought of my friend, gone by his own hand. I wondered if he had stood at a precipice like this. Not a physical one, but one equally daunting. If he had only known that beyond the pain, beyond the struggle, something waited. Something worth fighting for.

Reluctantly, I retreated. The safest option was to descend, cross several miles of heather-laden terrain, and approach Ben Nevis from its base. The detour was gruelling, sapping my remaining energy, but the thought of quitting never entered my mind.

When I finally began the climb up Ben Nevis, the zigzag path was buried under knee-deep snow. Every step was a battle, each movement draining what little strength I had left.

This was when I entered the pain cave. The mental and physical breaking point where you have to dig deeper than you ever thought possible. But I kept going, one step at a time, until at last, the summit was within reach.

When I stood atop Ben Nevis, I broke down. Tears streamed down my face as the weight of everything hit me—the grief, the pain, the triumph, the journey from that broken man on the tournament mat to this moment of victory. I had done it. I had conquered the ten highest peaks in the UK in just four days, covering over 100 kilometres and climbing nearly 7,000 metres.

The descent was no less harrowing. Exhausted and emotionally drained, I stumbled my way back to the forest line. Every cell in my body screamed at me to stop, but I pushed through, driven by the memory of why I was doing this. By the time I reached the van, I felt an unexpected burst of energy. Somehow, I found the strength to sprint the last 500 meters, collapsing into the back of the van with a mix of relief and disbelief.

I sat there and cried, thinking of my family's unwavering support, my friend, his family, and everyone who had lost someone to suicide. The money I had raised—over £2,500—would fund countless calls to Samaritans, giving others a chance to find hope in their darkest moments. That was why I had done it, not for personal glory, but to show that resilience was possible, that you could overcome even the deepest pain.

Now, when I placed the key in my barbershop door in the morning, the pride I felt wasn't just about business success. The familiar scents—aftershave, lemon, cleanliness—reminded me that life can continue after devastation, often in unexpected ways.

When clients sat in my chair and shared their struggles—their marriages ending, their businesses failing, their bodies betraying them—I recognised the look in their eyes. I've seen it in my mirror. I offer more than a haircut. I offer proof that the darkness passes, that resilience isn't something you're born with but something you build, one painful step at a time.

The mountains taught me that our greatest limitations exist in our minds. The path forward isn't about avoiding pain but moving through it with purpose. It's about understanding that when everything seems lost, when your body and spirit feel irreparably broken, you're actually at the starting line of your most important journey.

That's why I now speak at events about resilience, sharing not just my story but a framework for moving through life's darkest valleys. That's why I coach men, helping them rediscover their strength when they feel most weak.

Because I know the truth now: we don't become unbreakable by avoiding breaks. We become unbreakable by breaking open, by allowing ourselves to be vulnerable enough to heal.

If you're standing where I once stood—at the very edge of hope, wondering if the fight is worth it—reach out. The journey back isn't one you should walk alone. Together, we can find the strength that has always been inside you, waiting to be rediscovered.

Because no one should face their darkness alone.

Keys to Resilience:

1. **Acknowledge Your Pain and Vulnerability**
   Accept that feeling broken or vulnerable is not a sign of weakness but the first step toward healing.

2. **Don't Isolate Yourself—Seek Connection**
   Open up to friends, family, or professionals. Sharing your struggles can lessen the burden.

3. **Use Physical Activity as a Lifeline**
   Engage in exercise or challenging physical goals. Activities like running or hiking not only build strength but also release endorphins.

4. **Turn Setbacks into Growth Opportunities**
   Resilience isn't avoiding challenges but learning to embrace and grow from them.

5. **Set Meaningful Goals to Drive Recovery**
   Having a purpose, such as completing a marathon or raising awareness for a cause, can motivate you to move forward.

6. **Break Big Challenges into Manageable Steps**
   Focus on small, achievable tasks that contribute to larger goals.

7. **Find Role Models and Guidance**
   Look to others who have faced and overcome adversity.

8. **Raise Awareness and Help Others**
   By supporting causes like suicide prevention or mental health awareness, you gain purpose and healing.

9. **Accept the Power of Rest and Reflection**
   Allow yourself time to recover—physically and mentally.

10. **Remember You're Not Alone**
    Even when it feels like the weight of the world is on your shoulders, there are resources and people ready to help.

## ABOUT THE AUTHOR

# TONY HARESIGN

SCAN TO KNOW MORE

*Tony Haresign is a rare fusion of entrepreneur, cyber security specialist, and member of the Edinburgh Magic Circle, who channels decades of real world experience into transforming men's mental health. Having navigated his own struggles and experienced the devastating loss of friends, Tony brings profound authenticity to his mission. His unique background spans from barber chair confidant, where countless men found their voice to share their struggles, to boardroom strategist and stage performer. This multifaceted foundation, combined with his passion for mountain running, bikepacking, and kayaking, positions Tony as the mentor who truly understands the modern man's journey. He doesn't just speak about resilience -he embodies it, transforming vulnerability into strength through proven strategies and genuine connection.*

START OVER VOL 4

CHAPTER

# 4

# Rise of the Phoenix

BARRY CAREY

I stood at the edge of the Belfast road, the weight of existence crushing me from the inside out. The autumn wind bit at my face, but I barely felt it against the roaring emptiness within. One step. That's all it would take to end this pain. One step into oblivion.

This wasn't always my story. Before becoming the man who would survive the unsurvivable, I was just Barry Carey from Maguiresbridge, a tiny community in Northern Ireland where my father's dreams for me were as vast as the green countryside surrounding us. Born September 22, 1985, in Dublin's Rotunda Hospital, I I was given the name Barry, after the great Barry Mcguiga ,Irelands prize fighter who won the world title just months before my birth—my father's prophecy that I too would be a fighter, though neither of us could have imagined the battles that lay ahead.

The authentic Irish blood sustained me as I grew. My parents, Mary and John, along with my brother Owen and sisters Catherine and Colleen created our close-knit family of six. As you might guess, I was a little rascal from a very young age—you couldn't leave anything lying around, and you needed eyes in the back of your head to know where I was at all times.

My dad and I shared an incredibly strong bond from early on. The memory of his calloused hand engulfing mine as we walked to his truck still warms me. He would frequently take me on journeys in his lorry, pointing out landmarks and telling stories that made the landscape come alive. When he enrolled me in Judo classes, I understood even then that this wasn't just about sport—it was his way of ensuring no one would ever take advantage of his oldest son. His love was protective, fierce, and absolute.

## The Fall

The morning of July 12, 1995 started like any other summer day. Sunlight streamed through the kitchen window as I finished my breakfast, excited about playing football with friends later. Then came the knock. The sound still echoes in my memory—three sharp raps that somehow carried the weight of what was to come. When my mother opened the door, her face drained of colour so quickly it was as though someone had pulled a plug.

At nine years old, I stood frozen in our hallway as words like "accident" and "hospital" floated around me. My father—my hero, my protector, the man who drove me to Judo and taught me to stand tall—was gone at just 36 years old. I remember staring at his empty chair at dinner that night, my younger siblings too small to understand why Mammy couldn't stop crying, why our house suddenly felt hollow, like someone had scooped out its heart.

The following weeks blurred together. My school exams became meaningless scratches on paper. I wrote the answers mechanically while my mind screamed questions no teacher could answer: How do you become the man of the house when you're still a boy? How do you protect your family when you couldn't protect the one who mattered most?

The bullying started soon after. Perhaps the other children sensed my vulnerability, the way predators can smell fear. Some days I'd walk home with torn school clothes, other days with bruises cleverly placed where teachers wouldn't notice. My sister Colleen tells me I was greatly impacted, though many of these memories have mercifully faded from my conscious mind.

What remained instead was a crippling fear of death and extreme health anxiety. Every headache became a brain tumour, every stomach pain appendicitis. By fourteen, paranoia had wrapped its tentacles firmly around my mind. I became convinced that drugs were being slipped into my food at school, causing me harm. The fear grew so overwhelming that I began skipping school—first days, then weeks, then three months at a stretch.

My poor mother was at her wits' end. With a shop to run and three smaller children to care for on her own, my behaviour was yet another burden she couldn't possibly shoulder. Looking back now, I recognise her impossible position, though my teenage self couldn't comprehend the herculean effort it took for a widowed woman to keep our family afloat.

Eventually, she brought me to a counsellor who helped me get the treatment I desperately needed. Within a year, the cloud began to lift. At fifteen, I cautiously emerged from my shell, venturing out to socialise for the first time and discovering that I could still fit into the world. Football and Gaelic football offered salvation, giving me purpose and community when I needed it most. I threw myself into everything—sports, singing, acting, swimming. The accordion and guitar became outlets for emotions too complex for words.

At seventeen, I began a plumbing apprenticeship, though I never felt truly at ease in the trade. Anxiety still hovered at the edges of my confidence, making me fear mistakes and hesitate when learning new skills. I completed my qualification, but I'd never claim to be the world's most skilled plumber. Something else was waiting for me, though I couldn't yet see what it might be.

The Call to Adventure

"You should go to Australia," my mother and sister Colleen urged in 2008. A group of my friends were making the journey, and something about their encouragement sparked a longing for escape I hadn't recognised in myself.

Sydney welcomed me with blinding sunshine and endless possibility. The Opera House gleamed against the harbour like a promise, and Bondi's waves crashed in rhythmic invitation. The beaches and warm climate instantly drew me in, but it was the unexpected discovery of my talent for sales that truly opened my eyes to possibilities beyond the building industry.

I received a job offer selling vehicles that seemed too good to refuse. My intention was to return to Melbourne in early 2009 to pursue this career after spending the festive season with my Aunty Finola and Uncle Tim in Sydney. But life had other plans.

As my aunt showed me around Sydney's magnificent landmarks, the city cast its spell on me. The dazzling harbour, spectacular views, and vibrant energy captured my imagination completely. When I became involved in the Gaelic football scene and landed a construction job, my sales career ambitions were temporarily shelved.

Playing for Michael Cusacks GAA provided something I'd been searching for since losing my father—a home away from home. For the first time in years, I found friends who accepted me unconditionally, who laughed with me rather than at me. In Durty Nellys, a notorious Irish pub in Sydney, I became the team mascot, the centre of attention, the life of the party.

"Big Bad Bazza!" they'd cheer as I leapt atop the bar, microphone in one hand, pint in the other. The spotlight felt like salvation, each song and drink pushing away the shadows that had followed me across oceans. Three-day benders stretched into week-long disappearances from reality. I'd wake on unfamiliar couches, park benches, or apartment lobbies, mouth dry as desert sand, with only fractured memories of the night before.

Between blackouts and hangovers, a voice that sounded suspiciously like my father's whispered that I was wasting whatever he'd seen in me all those years ago. I silenced it with another round, another song, another embrace from strangers who knew nothing of the boy who'd lost everything on a July morning in Ireland.

I tried several times to straighten myself out. I even quit drinking for three months to prepare for my first amateur fight in 2011, which I regrettably lost. Predictably, I returned to drinking and partying, seeking comfort in familiar destructive patterns.

Then came 2013, when anxiety wrapped its familiar fingers around my throat in the middle of a construction site. I stood above a freshly dug trench, staring down into the dark rectangle of earth, and found myself wishing someone would push me in and cover me up. The ground swayed beneath my work boots, and suddenly I couldn't remember how to breathe.

"Baz, we'll fight through this together." Mark's arm around my shoulders anchored me to the present as tears carved paths through the worksite dust on my face. His words cut through the fog: "We'll get you the help you need."

That night, I poured every bottle down the sink, watching amber liquid disappear like years of my life. The smell burned my nostrils, a funeral pyre for "Big Bad Bazza." In its place stood just Barry—terrified, broken, but finally ready to draw that line in the sand.

Finding a New Path

I needed to replace old habits with something healthier, something that could provide the rush I craved without the devastating aftermath. My sister Colleen and good friend Chrissy had been encouraging me to try running for years, but I'd always been more interested in drinking with the lads and meeting women.

In 2013, I finally took their advice and registered for my first race. Somehow, despite my lifestyle, I found myself at the starting line of a marathon—the ultimate test of physical and mental endurance. What possessed me to attempt such a gruelling event as my introduction to running remains a mystery, but that decision changed everything.

My first marathon came after months of dawn runs, each footfall a rejection of the man I'd been. At kilometre 35, when my legs burned with lactic acid and every breath felt like inhaling fire, I found a strange clarity. The pain was clean, honest—nothing like the self-destruction I'd practiced for years. Crossing the finish line, legs trembling and lungs heaving, I experienced a rush more powerful than any alcohol had ever provided—pure, earned euphoria flooding every cell.

The running bug bit hard. I joined a running group led by the incredible Keith Hong, not realising I'd soon be training alongside Olympic and Commonwealth Games athletes. Ben St Lawrence—Australian record holder with a 10km time of 27 minutes and 24 seconds that seemed superhuman—became both mentor and measuring stick. His breathing barely changed during intervals that left me gasping, hands on knees. "You've got more," he'd say simply, and somehow I'd find it.

Harry Summers, a three-time City 2 Surf Champion and Commonwealth Games representative, showed me what raw talent combined with discipline could achieve. Ollie Hoare, who later became a world-class miler and Commonwealth gold medallist, demonstrated the relentless work ethic required at the highest levels. I couldn't have written a better screenplay for my redemption if I'd tried.

The transformation happened almost without my noticing. Morning runs replaced hangovers. Recovery shakes replaced pints. Race medals accumulated where empty bottles once stood. My body became a machine I respected rather than punished, each personal best a stepping stone away from the abyss.

Within months, I finished in the top 50 of the City 2 Surf, one of the world's largest fun runs with 85,000 participants, completing the 14 kilometres in 48 minutes. In 2015, I stood at the start line of the Sydney 10km, ankle freshly healed but heavily strapped after snapping a ligament two weeks earlier. The doctor had advised against racing, but something more powerful than medical wisdom propelled me forward. When the gun fired, I channelled every painful memory into each stride. The rhythm of feet hitting pavement became a meditation: I am not what happened to me. I am what I choose to become. I finished in the top 20 with a personal best of 34 minutes—Irish resilience and grit carrying me across the line.

My life had found new purpose, but the social aspects still presented challenges. Explaining to others why I didn't drink often resulted in questioning looks or outright disbelief. On my 30th birthday, after three years of sobriety, I considered allowing myself one celebratory blowout. Thankfully, my sister Colleen talked me out of it. And thank God for the genius who invented non-alcoholic beer, because I genuinely missed the taste of a cold pint.

In 2017, life brought another major change when my coach Sean Williams moved to Melbourne. I loved that man to bits. He filled my mind with the grit, belief and determination it took to succeed in Athletics and in life in general. He was the Alex Ferguson of Athletics. After training alone for a while in Sydney, I visited Melbourne for a weekend to see what I thought of it. The city's renowned running trails and beautiful scenery captivated me immediately. With characteristic spontaneity, I packed up my nine-year life in Sydney and moved to Melbourne the following week to reunite the bond with my amazing coach Sean.

## The Darkest Night

Looking back, I made several decisions that didn't prioritise my mental health and wellbeing. My mother had instilled in me a powerful work ethic, and I rarely took days off even from jobs I hated. I never turned down extra hours or shifts, fearing I might disappoint someone. This led to gruelling schedules—working more than 60 hours weekly in construction while running up to 140 kilometres. I'd rise at 3 a.m. for my first run of the day, then work a full shift, followed by another training session.

I was a beast, pushing my body to extremes and running on sheer determination. But in 2018, the candle I'd been burning at both ends finally consumed me. I suffered an acute fracture in my pelvis that left me on crutches, unable to work, with no income. Debt mounted quickly, and Australia's high cost of living meant I nearly became homeless. I remember walking around with just $3 to my name, unable to afford dental care for two painful abscesses. In desperation, I extracted the teeth myself and signed up for welfare—something I'd sworn I'd never do.

Few people understand how challenging life as an elite athlete can be, especially in a sport like distance running where funding is minimal and most competitors work full-time jobs alongside their training. Unlike premier league footballers with their support systems and salaries, athletes in my position were constantly choosing between training, recovery, work, and basic survival.

Despite everything, I refused to quit. I dragged myself two kilometres to the gym daily on crutches, determined to maintain fitness however possible. I discovered the ergometer, a hand cycle that allowed me to continue cardiovascular training while my pelvis healed. Six months later, in July 2019, I shattered my 10km personal best by a full minute, clocking 33 minutes, and set a new 5km personal best of 16 minutes.

I'd learned to balance my training with better recovery and strength work, recognising that my sympathetic nervous system had been constantly overactive. But just as things were improving, disaster struck again. While working in July 2019, I suffered a severe accident. My finger was nearly severed, my hand rendered useless, and the trauma triggered the most severe mental collapse of my life.

Following the accident, I was diagnosed with Post-Traumatic Stress Disorder. Unable to work and increasingly unwell, I flew to San Francisco to visit my godmother Teresa, hoping a change of scenery might provide comfort. But as they say, wherever you go, you take your mind with you.

San Francisco's fog matched my mental state—thick, impenetrable, disorienting. The Golden Gate Bridge called to me with a deadly siren song. My godmother did everything possible to help, holding my hand as we crossed streets, connecting me with support groups and psychologists. Nothing worked. Eventually, we decided I should return to Ireland where my family could help.

The Abyss

I arrived home in early 2020, unaware that the world was about to face its greatest crisis in generations. As COVID-19 spread globally, killing millions and forcing lockdowns, my already fragile mental state deteriorated further. The isolation and fear only amplified my depression, which had become so severe I struggled to get out of bed or shower. When I attempted to run—once my salvation—I felt as though I carried the weight of the world on my shoulders.

The morning of April 2020 began with a heaviness that made even breathing seem laborious. I moved through our family home like a ghost, barely registering my surroundings. In the kitchen, I reached for a knife, the metal cool against my palm. The decision wasn't rational—it was the desperate act of someone who couldn't bear another moment of mental anguish. As I raised the blade to my throat, my sister's scream pierced the moment. My mother nearly collapsed as my sister knocked the knife from my hand, the clatter against the floor tiles startling me back to reality.

I checked myself into treatment in Omagh, Northern Ireland immediately after this incident. The ten weeks that followed were among the most difficult of my life. Though broken, I somehow found the strength to run when nurses deemed it safe to release me from the ward. With professional help and medication adjustments, I gradually stabilised enough to return home and take on part-time work at a local food factory. Morning walks became part of my routine, and life slowly began to improve.

But the fragile peace didn't last. On October 28, 2020, the darkness descended again, heavier than before. I called my brother Owen in England, telling him I wasn't feeling myself—that I felt like a lost soul with no place in this world. "Barry, depression is difficult to manage," he reassured me, "but your feelings will pass." I tried to find comfort in his words.

The morning of October 30th, 2020 dawned grey and heavy with mist. At breakfast, the weight I'd been carrying finally crushed me completely. Something about the mundane normalcy—butter melting into toast, the kettle's whistle, my mother's gentle morning chatter—made the contrast with my internal darkness unbearable. Tears came without warning, hot and unstoppable.

"What's up, son?" My mother's face creased with concern.

"I don't know, Mum. I just...I can't carry this anymore." The emptiness inside me had grown so vast it seemed to echo.

"Go for a run," she suggested. "It always helps."

I nodded, laced up my shoes, and headed out the familiar road toward Belfast. The countryside unfolded around me—green fields that had witnessed generations of Irish suffering and survival. My ancestors had endured famine, war, and hardship, yet somehow their resilience had skipped over me, leaving me hollow.

My thoughts spiralled darker with each kilometre. What was the point of continuing? I'd never get my life straight. Never find love. Eventually, I'd drive away everyone who cared about me. The traffic increased as I approached a busier section, lorries thundering past with mechanical indifference. One step. That's all it would take.

I don't remember making the decision, only the momentary sensation of weightlessness before impact erased everything.

Resurrection

Consciousness returned in fragments—bright lights, urgent voices, the antiseptic smell of hospital, my mother's hand gripping mine so tightly it hurt. Her face appeared above me, eyes red-rimmed but fierce with love.

"Did you try to commit suicide?" she asked, voice steady despite everything.

The shame burned hotter than my injuries. "Yes, Mum. I did. I was in so much pain. I couldn't bear it anymore."

Her hand stroked my hair like she had when I was small. "Son, I love you so much. You are strong, and we will get through this together. I'm your mother, and we'll do everything we can."

In that moment, broken in every way a person can break—body shattered, spirit crushed, dignity stripped by the need for nurses to feed and clean me—I understood something crucial: If a lorry couldn't take me out of this world, perhaps I wasn't meant to leave it yet.

My time in the Belfast Royal was the most difficult few weeks of my life. Physical pain from my injuries competed with the emotional agony of confronting what I'd done. One lung was damaged, making each breath a struggle. The prospect of a wheelchair-bound future seemed both punishment and challenge.

Recovery began with the smallest victories. The first time I managed to drag myself from bed to shower felt like climbing Everest. My arms trembled with the effort of supporting my weight, pain shooting through damaged nerves, but the warm water on my face was worth every excruciating inch of progress.

After treatment at Belfast Royal, I returned to Omagh for another difficult six weeks. In the psychiatric ward, I found myself surrounded by others fighting invisible battles. Their faces reflected different versions of my own pain—some vacant, some contorted with internal struggles, some flickering with the same desperate hope I was nurturing. We were all broken vessels trying to hold light.

I began rebuilding my mind with the same disciplined approach I'd once applied to training. Reading became my mental intervals, writing songs my recovery jogs, and setting small goals my long runs. Neuroplasticity became my mantra—rewiring neural pathways that had once led only to darkness, creating new routes toward light.

The cold shower practice began as an act of desperation. One particularly bleak morning when medications and therapy felt insufficient, I remembered something about the Wim Hof method and turned the shower temperature to its coldest setting. The shock of icy water sent electricity through my nervous system, jerking me fully into the present moment. For thirty seconds, there was no past trauma, no uncertain future—only the sharp, immediate reality of cold against skin. I gasped, cursed, and emerged feeling more alive than I had in months.

Each day, I stayed under the frigid spray a few seconds longer. The practice became ritual, then medicine. Cold water therapy rewired something fundamental in my approach to discomfort—teaching me that temporary pain could be walked through rather than avoided, that resilience grows in the space between impulse and reaction.

By Christmas 2020, the wheelchair gathered dust in a corner as I took wobbly steps around my mother's kitchen, the smell of her traditional Irish stew filling the house. The familiar holiday rituals felt like welcome benchmarks of normality, though nothing about me felt normal anymore. I had died in one way and been reborn in another—the same Barry but fundamentally altered, carrying both more weight and more wisdom.

"Where could we go today?" I asked my mother one January morning, restlessness humming through my healing bones. "How about we climb Cuilcagh Mountain?"

She looked at me like I'd suggested flying to the moon. "Barry, are you fucking mad? You're in a leg brace. No fucking way."

Her reaction only strengthened my resolve. The following week, I convinced my friend Aaron to take me to the Mayo Cliffs instead. Each step up the narrow, steep path sent pain shooting through my damaged leg, but also satisfaction. The wind whipped stronger as we climbed, carrying the scent of earth and sea. At the summit, I stood breathless, surveying the vastness of Fermanagh spread below me, and knew with absolute certainty that I was back—different, but stronger.

Twelve weeks after my injury, my physiotherapist cleared me to begin a walk/jog programme, and I returned to what I loved. Everyone, including myself, was astonished by the speed of my recovery. In 2021, I worked in factories in England while continuing my comeback to athletics. My brother Owen's support and occasional tough love gave me additional strength and motivation.

My healing regimen expanded beyond physical therapy. Cold showers, breathing exercises, journaling, inner spiritual work, and reading all contributed significantly to my emotional and physical recovery. I embraced discomfort, discovering that pushing through difficulty strengthened both body and mind in unexpected ways.

Return With the Elixir

In May 2021, I felt ready to return to Australia—the land where I'd experienced both destruction and growth. This time, I arrived with purpose and determination to build something meaningful from the ashes of my past.

Four years later, I sit in a Sydney café, autumn sunshine warming my face through the window. The city bustles outside—the same streets where I once stumbled drunk, where I later pushed my body to athletic limits, and where I now walk with a purpose that transcends both extremes.

The journey back to Australia wasn't just geographical—it represented returning to the scene of my former destruction and rewriting the story. My body, once broken beyond recognition, now carries me through 34-minute 10Ks and 16-minute 5Ks. I've claimed seventh place in Sydney's premier race and shattered the Western Sydney 5K record by more than a minute.

But numbers and rankings no longer define my worth. The true measure of my resurrection lies elsewhere: in the faces of those who attend my speaking events, their eyes reflecting recognition of their own struggles; in the peaceful determination of my ice bath students as they learn to embrace discomfort; in the steps I took alongside my friend with stage 5 kidney disease during our 100-kilometre charity walk.

The phoenix doesn't just rise from ashes—it uses the very fire that destroyed it to fuel its rebirth. My superpower wasn't running or resilience or even survival. My superpower was ADHD—the very condition that had once contributed to my struggles now gives me the hyperfocus and boundless energy to help others find their way back from darkness.

My message is simple but forged in the crucible of experience: Mindset is everything. The things we tell ourselves become our reality. Faith and hope aren't abstract concepts but practical tools for survival. And no matter how completely you've been shattered, there is a path back to wholeness that only you can walk, guided by those who've travelled similar terrain.

To those still suffering in silence: I see you. I was you. The darkness you're experiencing isn't terminal—it's the necessary contrast that will eventually make your light burn brighter. Hold on. Reach out. The hand that pulls you back from the edge might be scarred, but that's how you'll know it's strong enough to carry you until you can walk on your own.

The universe has a plan for each of us. My journey from broken boy to "Big Bad Bazza" to broken man to mental health warrior wasn't random—it was preparation. Every step, even those toward destruction, led me here: to this moment, to this message, to the opportunity to help you find your spark again.

What's your superpower? Let's discover it together.

## ABOUT THE AUTHOR

# BARRY CAREY

SCAN TO KNOW MORE

*Barry Carey is a dedicated health and fitness coach, mental health ambassador, and qualified mental health first aider. With over 12 years as an elite distance runner, he combines his athletic experience with a passion for wellness. As a public speaker and qualified tradesman, Barry shares insights into resilience and recovery. A suicide survivor himself, he leverages his strengths in breathwork and cold water exposure to promote mental and spiritual clarity. Committed to shining a light on those facing mental health challenges, Barry inspires others to confront their demons and embrace healing, fostering a supportive community for all.*

*For more information or to book a free and confidential video zoom call, contact:* *Recoveryplus@gmail.com*

START OVER VOL 4

CHAPTER

# 5

# One Breath Away

LISA LESTER

From Near Death to Miraculous Survival through the Power of Prayer & Faith

Breathing
January 7, 2018

Fog so thick, I can't tell whether I'm seeing with my eyes or imagination. Surrounded by floating white curtains. Alone. No sense of where I am.

It comes to me that I'm lying on my side, immobilised by numbing tiredness. A heavy soup of confusion slows my thinking. I hear someone speaking in low tones and try to call out, but my voice won't come.

Where am I?

Mechanical noises. Murmuring voices. Measured beeping.

A hospital. Dear Lord, please help me. I'm trapped in a body that won't allow me to sit up, eyes that won't focus. A woman is talking to someone on the other side of the curtains.

"She had a ruptured brain aneurysm and she's quadriplegic."

The words kick the wind out of me. That can't be me. That just can't be me. I'm the mother of a teenage boy and I can't be paralysed. I'm the only parent he has.

Somehow, I find strength to wiggle my fingers, then toes. I force down panic and take stock. No casts. Something ticklish on my face. Head, sore. I concentrate, inching my hand up to investigate. First discovery: oxygen tube under my nose. My fingers creep along to find a hose coming out of my head.

Oh my God. Someone has cut a hole in my skull and stuck a tube in. Shock burns through me but I'm too weak for tears. My fingertips tap their way to something that feels like a zipper at the edge of my hairline, along the side of my head and around the back.

My head has been split open and stapled back together. Now tears come. Staples. Tubes. Surgery. Whatever caused this was major.

But I'm alive.

I need to fill my lungs with oxygen like in my opera training days. Breathe in deeply to smell the spring flowers. Blow out gently over the hot chocolate.

A deadening fatigue overpowers me. I think of deep healing breaths but sleep comes to take me away. Breathe in. Breathe out. Thank you, God, for keeping me breathing.

Presley

Three Days Earlier

It's the last Thursday before school starts after Christmas break and there is a magnificent display of ice castles downtown at The Forks.

"Let's go make a memory," I announced. Presley has heard me say this a thousand times.

At 15, I'm sure he would've been happier to go out with friends, but he didn't want to disappoint me. I promised we wouldn't stay long. The mayor would be there and the editor at the magazine I work for wanted pictures.

January in Winnipeg is bitterly cold and bright in daytime, snow sparkling like diamonds at night.

Long before Europeans arrived, The Forks was an important gathering place for Indigenous people. When I visit, I imagine their songs, drums, and feathered headdresses around the fire, shaping part of my spiritual Metis ancestry.

My father's side is British, but my mother's roots are French-Canadian voyageurs. My sweet Memere, shared how Manitoba got its name from the haunting sound of waves at Lake Manitoba, believed to be the Great Spirit, Manitou. The story is meaningful to me, as my faith has always been central to my life and how I raise my son.

Presley and I made our way to the brightly lit walls of ice with high hopes for an exciting 2018, including my latest passion project developing a health tech company.

Presley dreams of being a goalie for the New York Rangers. In the midst of a winning AAA hockey season, he was pumped about the upcoming tournament in Minneapolis.

As we walked, a wave of dizziness hit me and I stopped to steady myself.

Presley side-eyed me. "Are you okay Mom?"

"I'm fine. Just a little woozy. I think I might be coming down with the flu."

I smiled my way around the ice castles, chatted with the Mayor, and snapped pictures, fighting back a sense of vertigo. But Presley saw right through me. He tipped his head toward the exit. "I think we should get home so I can do my English essay. Hockey practice tomorrow."

We left, not knowing that two nights later, I'd be lying on a gurney fighting for my life.

Saturday

I had been feeling off for weeks, constantly fatigued, with intermittent headaches and blurry vision. I had desperately prayed to fix what was wrong.

By Saturday morning, nothing much had changed – but I had big plans that night. My brother Dan was taking Presley to his hockey game. While I normally never miss a game, I'd been invited to sing for a birthday at a popular nightclub.

The prospect of cancelling was upsetting, as replacing a singer at the last minute is a real hassle.

Running through my vocal exercises was rough going. Leaning over the kitchen counter, I called the show producer.

"Hi, John, it's Lisa."

"Hey, how ya doing?"

Before I could answer, he jumped in. "You aren't calling to tell me you're not coming tonight, are you? I've had two people back out because of the flu. Tell me you don't have the flu."

"No, no!" I forced a laugh. "I'm just calling to find out what time you want me."

"Good! Because if you're gonna cancel, I'm gonna be totally pissed."

Weeks later, I told John he may have saved my life. Had I stayed home alone with no one to help me, I might have died before Presley got home.

I rested through the day but nothing changed.

"Mom, are you ready?" Presley called, as he dragged his gear to the front door. "Uncle Dan texted he's on his way. I need you now!"

As before every game, we joined together in prayer to ask God and our heavenly angels to protect all the players from injury and help his team bring home a victory. A quick hug and he was off.

The club was packed. Greeting everyone, I smiled through the soreness spiking up my neck.

The first band started and people were on their feet dancing and singing. Soon it was time for our set. Enthusiastic applause lifted my spirits as I took the microphone and the Rod Hussey Revue dove into the opening notes of CCR "Have You Ever Seen the Rain?" I encouraged the audience to sing along, the pain in my neck worsening. As we reached the closing notes, I felt a sharp piercing bolt and suddenly the whole room was tilted and spinning.

Terrified, I grabbed the microphone stand to keep from falling, turning toward the band.

"Something's wrong," I said. "I don't feel well."

The bass player came to me and yelled, "Grab my coat." I held on tightly, willing my legs to keep moving. He played me off stage to a vacant booth, where I slid onto the bench.

"Are you okay?" His eyes searched for truth in my fake smile.

"I'll be fine!" I managed to say. "Go back and finish the set."

I gripped my head with both hands, trying to stop the pain and dizziness. The music boomed as if through an amplifier. All my senses had intensified. The rising smell of beer was followed by an overwhelming wave of nausea.

A guy – manager or bouncer – all business and bluster, rapped his knuckles on the table and yelled, "Okay, I need this booth now. Let's go. Move!"

He dragged me onto a chair like a ragdoll and wrenched it across the floor to a back room, wooden legs screeching, my head pounding with every torturous bump.

"I'll find your friends to take you home," he shouted, releasing the chair with a thunk.

The impact sent shock waves through my head. I crumpled in agony.

Then, like an angel, a woman knelt beside me. "Are you all right, Lisa?" she asked.

"No, I'm not." I started to cry. "This terrible headache came on suddenly and I think I'm going to be sick."

"I'm Violet, I'm a nurse," she said, handing me an empty ice bucket. "I watched you leave the stage." Her face lined with concern, she took my pulse.

John, the producer, came in and his face froze. "Hey Lisa, I heard you're sick.

What's going on?"

"My head feels like I was hit with a baseball bat and struck with a hot poker in my neck."

The nurse's eyes met mine with sobering urgency. "I think you should get to the Hospital."

"Okay," my voice jammed in my throat. "Call 911. And my mom. I can't dial."

"I'll do it." John pulled out his phone.

Violet placed a bag of ice gently on the back of my head and neck. She put an arm around me as I vomited.

"The ambulance is coming, John's voice boomed, "and I talked to your Mom. She called Dan."

I looked up and John's expression made me realize I was in real trouble. I feared never seeing my son again and tears streamed down my face.

"I'm right here with you, Lisa," Violet said in her steady, soothing voice. "I'm staying right here to wait for the ambulance. Just stay with me."

"Oh my God," I whispered. "Am I dying?"

As I Lay Dying

I'm clinging to the thought that once Dan and the ambulance arrive, everything will be fine. Senses heightened. Stabbing light. Music, shouting, laughter – all at ear-splitting intensity.

What I didn't know then was that I'd suffered a ruptured brain aneurysm and chances of surviving were slim without accurate diagnosis and prompt treatment. Fact: Half die shortly afterwards; two thirds of survivors have permanent problems and disabilities. All I knew then was that I was in pretty rough shape and failing quickly.

"Is it alright if I pray?" Violet asked, holding me so I wouldn't fall off the chair.

I nodded. "Thank you." I pushed past my tears.

As our words united in a cry for help, I thought, "Please, God help me get through this."

I was terrified and getting ever weaker. I could think only of Presley. If I died, he'd be an orphan. Who would keep him safe and guide him through the challenges of life as a teenager and young adult?

I prayed as hard as I could, over and over, "Dear God in heaven, help me get back to my boy."

Then something so incredibly beautiful happened. All the ugliness and noise of the room fell away and I felt as though I'd been lifted into a sweet-smelling place, free from pain and terror.

A gentle breeze caressed my face. The strength of great love flowed through every fibre of my being.

In the darkness, I saw a distant light. As it neared, my sense of peace grew deeper.

Someone was reaching for me. I ached with joy at the sight of those familiar rosy cheeks, that big smile. It was my loving Dad, shining brightly in his own light.

He came closer, brimming with happiness.

""Why are you here?" I asked.

"Lisa, it's going to be okay," he said. He opened his arms and I understood. He was telling me heaven was going to be fine. I yearned to go with him, to hold him, heaven drawing me in.

But I stopped myself. "Please, don't touch me" I said, knowing I had to be firm, my answer clear. "I have to stay with Presley. I love you Dad, but I can't go with you."

Radiating comfort and love, my Dad let me know I need not be afraid because he was with me and told me I will be ok. Don't worry. His strength lifted me, protected me. I needed to "let go and let God." I immersed myself in love and bliss.

Someone was calling my name, cradling my hand tenderly.

"Lisa, can you hear me?"

The distant voice gradually became clearer.

"Lisa, it's me, Dan. Are you awake?"

I wanted to be with Dad, basking in the serene warmth of his light. But the voice calling me was insistent. I was plunged back into reality: pounding music, bright lights and the stench of beer. I felt the weight of my body, the searing pain in my head.

"Danny?"

"Yes, it's me." He held my hand to his face.

"Look! Dad is here," I said. "Can you see him?"

"Dad? Here?"

I opened my eyes. Dad was gone. I started to whimper, his loss a fresh grief. "He was just here."

I could see the fear in my brother's eyes. "Okay. That means Dad's here to help."

He asked Violet about the ambulance, shocked it hadn't arrived.

"We're still waiting," she said. "It's been almost an hour."

Eventually, I remember Dan leading a parade of paramedics into that smelly room, then questions thundering down on me. Vomiting for how long? What kind of headache? Food? Drink? Drugs?

Dan helped me into my coat, urging them to get me into the ambulance.

"There's no room on the street up front. We have to use the back lane," said the paramedic. "And we can't get a stretcher in here."

In the end, Dan half-carried me out through the rear entrance leaning me up against a garbage bin until the ambulance appeared.

They placed me on the stretcher and wrapped me in blankets. I prayed my thanks. It was just about midnight, almost two hours since I left the stage.

"Which hospital?" Dan called out to the driver. "I'll meet you there."

"We don't know yet," he answered. "We need to be assigned a hospital."

We waited through yet one more delay while the ambulance idled.

"We're going to Saint Boniface," the driver yelled. That decision, I learned months later, could have cost me my life. Only the Health Sciences Centre could accommodate the treatment I would ultimately need.

"I'll be there with Presley and Mom as quickly as I can." Danny squeezed my hand then scooted out of the ambulance. "You'll be fine. You're in good hands."

I knew I was. I was in God's hands.

At the Saint Boniface Hospital ER, drop-offs were confined to single lane access, forcing drivers to line up and wait their turn to unload.

They placed me on the gurney in the foyer with automatic doors opening to the -40 frigid winter weather.

"They'll see you soon," said an ambulance attendant. Soon never arrived. But my family did.

I was getting colder and colder until mom found some heated blankets to comfort me. Immediately, Dan went off to get me processed.

Presley kissed my forehead and held my hand. Bolstered by his quiet strength, I allowed myself to cry. When I told him about seeing his Grandpa, he nodded as if he already knew. I so badly wanted to close my eyes but was terrified that, if I drifted off, I might never wake up.

The waiting was endless. I'd left the stage shortly before 10pm. I finally saw a doctor at 2am. Then there were more delays.

After a CT scan, I was sent for another test.

My mother was weak with exhaustion, and Presley, tired after a hard hockey game, could hardly keep his eyes open.

"You two go home and get some rest" said Dan. I'll call when we know the results.

These people are experts and will know how to help her."

At 5:00 am Dan reported my diagnosis: a subarachnoid hemorrhage, a brain bleed. They were sending me to the Health Sciences Centre for surgery.

"We'll be waiting for you after surgery," he assured me. "Everything will be fine."

Exhausted, I closed my eyes and thought of Dad, his comforting arms. He promised it was going to be OK.

I was no longer afraid. It was as if the prayers of those around me were vibrating through my very soul. I was surrounded by angels, our heavenly Father caring for my every need.

Dan called Mom and told her that neurosurgeon, Dr. Anthony Kaufmann, would be operating at 7 am.

"The nurses all said he's among the best in the country"

"Surgery," Mom said and Dan waited through her silence as she steadied herself.

Surgery

Craniotomy is a scary word. I'm glad I never heard it until I had one. If open heart surgery sounds life-threatening, open skull surgery sounds like a horror movie.

I knew nothing about brain aneurysms before this. And unfortunately, no one around me that night seemed to know the symptoms of a brain bleed. Not the paramedics or the first people who saw me at Saint Boniface Hospital. Not even Violet the nurse.

At my surgery follow-up, Dr. Kaufmann explained that 75 percent of the time, lives could be saved if the public recognized the symptoms of a brain aneurysm as readily as they do signs of a heart attack or stroke.

"A ruptured brain aneurysm is typically more of a leak than a burst," he said. "A bleed of merely a few seconds could cause the patient to go into a coma. Longer and the person will die."

It is essential that anyone with a ruptured brain aneurysm get to a hospital quickly for diagnosis and treatment. Otherwise, a second – often deadly – bleed may follow within hours or days.

Almost 10 hours passed between my rupture and surgery. I could have easily slipped into a coma or died while waiting in the ER.

In the neurosurgery waiting room, Dan had no idea what to expect.

Desperate for information, he searched my condition online. Life threatening. Permanent brain damage. Immediate treatment essential. The phrases heightened his concern, particularly after all the long delays getting me into surgery. Would I make it? Would I be able to walk or talk again?

Shuddering, he closed his eyes and asked God to see me safely through surgery.

It was now 13 hours since my aneurysm had ruptured. According to his research, I had a one in six chance to come out without major repercussions. The words "successful recovery" ran in a loop through his mind.

The one recollection I have about my surgery sits in that fuzzy part of my mind between true memory and something else. It was a profoundly spiritual moment.

I remember looking down on myself in the center of a blue and white room. A large team was working on me, maybe six or eight people. Order and calm, everyone moving with purpose.

I could hear murmuring but can't recall the words.

Unafraid, I watched the scene below. It was as if my eyes were a camera, zooming in to see what the surgeon and his assistants could see. Everything was draped and covered, except where my skull had been opened. It was not at all unnerving and I could recall every meticulous detail of the surgery. I was so intrigued I needed to watch again. Twice. I could feel my Dad with the team of angels all around me.

Then memory fades.

Dan sat alone in the waiting room. When,shortly after 1:00 pm, Dr. Kaufmann came in with a drawn expression, his heart filled with dread. "Let's go into the hallway" the doctor told him. "Just for privacy. Lisa's in recovery."

Dan covered his face with his hands and sobbed. "Thank God."

"Lisa's aneurysm was in the back of her head. The surgery was successful and she's now in the step-down unit, so we can keep close watch."

"Will she be okay? Why did the surgery take so long?"

"Every aneurysm is different. Hers was an unusual shape and in a challenging location. It took time to ensure we could properly secure it so it won't re-bleed.

She'll stay in the hospital for at least two weeks, where we will be keeping a close eye on her progress, then reassess"

He outlined the risks I faced in the next few days: vasospasm, which can lead to ischemic stroke, a blood clot cutting off oxygen to the brain; and hydrocephalus, an accumulation of fluid that can cause brain damage. A tube out of my temple now served as a drain.

He warned Dan that I would be very tired and sensitive to sounds, so to keep family visits brief and quiet. To aid healing and reduce risk of infection there were strict rules. No visitors outside of immediate family. No flowers. No excitement. No drama. Two-weeks post-op they would determine if I needed further hospital care like physical and speech therapy before resuming life at home.

Home. What would that mean? Dan braced against the hard unknown.

"But she's okay? She did fine in the surgery, right?"

Dr. Kaufmann gave a tired smile. "We almost lost her twice. She was under anesthesia a very long time which is hard on the body, but yes, she tolerated the surgery well."

"That's our Lisa." Dan shook Dr. Kaufmann's hand and left to give Presley and Mom the good news.

Through the lingering fog of drugs that kept me alive during surgery, I saw Presley come to my side. In my altered reality, we hugged and I held him close. I had no idea whether I'd be able to walk normally, but knew I could think. Somehow,

I'd find my way back to being me, or whatever the "new me" was going to be.

All I know for sure – and deeply appreciate – is that after surgery, my family rallied around me.

Months later Mom told me, "Lisa, after the operation, you could barely move. You didn't talk. We had no idea if you even could. Tubes were coming out of you, all kinds of monitors attached. But you recognised us and that gave us such a lift.

You were so weak, barely able to open your eyes. Presley touched your face and told you how happy he was to see you, how he needed you to get well. Within minutes you fell asleep and he sat there quietly for hours, just holding your hand."

The strength of my family's love supported me, relaying the full impact of the Lord's answer to all our prayers. With his help I had survived the worst of my ordeal and was going to get better.

Thank God John had called and pushed me to go sing that night. Thank God my brother Dan was home. And thank God I didn't die waiting for surgery.

God had heard all of those prayers during that long harrowing night and had taken care of me.

I'd survived the operation, but was still far from going home. "Touch and go." "Wait and see." "Not out of the woods yet."

I woke up to my Mom sitting in the chair beside the bed. She patted my hand, oddly pleased when she first heard me speak.

After being completely immobilised, every minor improvement was a big deal. Sitting up in bed for the first time. Being able to sip water and eat a cracker. I was weak but my arms and my brain worked. When the entire family came in to visit, they talked in hushed voices and moved on tiptoe. Presley kissed me on the forehead. "Why'd you guys look so glum? You'd think I'd been hit by a truck or something," I said.

My younger brother Curtis had come in from Calgary.

"Listen to you!" he said. "You're talking so much better than yesterday."

Presley's whole face lit up. "Are you feeling better, Mom?"

"A little stronger, yes."

I could feel their relief. Still, I remained bedridden, hooked up to tubes, drips, drains and wires monitoring every breath and heartbeat.

Raising a Vibration

In those early days, overpowered by tiredness, I still had a deep sense I was going to make it, that I was inching back to being myself. What helped most is my belief in the power of prayer. I was deeply moved to learn that many people outside my circle of family and friends were praying for me.

A whole community was raising a vibration. I felt like I was floating, walking on a bridge of halos. All those beautiful words and heartfelt prayers were lifting me, protecting me, helping me heal.

Healing from brain surgery is fraught with risk, occasional setbacks and many hurdles. Preventing infection is top priority, along with watching for signs of potential complications.

Day and night, the nurses were quick to check out the smallest warning from the monitors and evaluate any changes in behaviour that might be signs of neurological impairment or imbalance.

Healing a Brain

Healing a brain that has suffered a traumatic injury from an accident or a ruptured aneurysm requires a lot of special care.

When therapy began to get me ready to walk, I knew it wasn't going to be as simple as swinging my legs off the bed and standing. I was grateful to have a team endowed with both expertise and ample compassion. Reassuring hands supported me as I steadied myself against the shrieking ache in my legs.

Getting out of bed meant freedom. I was determined to make it to that lady's room on my own steam! I took a step, planted my foot. It held. Then another. Mom was right there watching.

"Way to go!" she applauded. For one brief moment I was 14 again with a baton spinning over my head, my hair flying like a horse's mane as I twirled it behind my back, Mom cheering me on from the stands.

When Presley came in for one of his regular visits, I proudly showed off my new leg compressor routine. We both laughed and then the briefest shadow clouded his eyes. I knew that look.

"I need to ask you something," he said, his eyes gripping mine. "You can say no. It's Fine."

He dropped his head. "The tournament in Minneapolis."

"Oh no! What day is it, did you miss it?"

"No. We leave tomorrow," he said, then caught himself. "I mean they leave tomorrow.

I'll stay home."

"Why aren't you going? Do you need me to get you a ride?"

"I've got one. Mr. Lisi arranged everything. Remember? But Uncle Dan and Grandma think it's a bad idea for me to go to Minneapolis right now." He ducked his head to hide his tears.

"Because of me?"

He bobbed his head.

My heart quaked.

"Oh Presley! I'm so sorry you have to go through all of this. You go play hockey. I need you to be a boy and be with your friends. Having you sit at home worrying about me isn't good for either of us. Tell anyone who asks that I'm doing well and I insisted you play, because that's the truth. Go get packed, Presley. Play hard and bring your mama a win!"

Balancing Act

After Presley left for Minneapolis, a frightening development sent new shockwaves through my family. As I was telling my mother how much I'd love a hamburger, she suddenly looked stunned.

I'd lost my ability to talk. Although I was convinced I was speaking perfectly formed words and sentences, Mom was hearing mumbo jumbo.

A CT scan revealed elevated cerebral spinal fluid (CSF) levels in my brain. The brain continuously manufactures CFS to bring nutrients and carry off waste. If not absorbed normally, pressure builds inside the cranium, interfering with brain function such as speech. Hence, the drainage tube in my head. It's a delicate balancing act closely watched by the medical team. A treatment adjustment was made and my speaking improved.

Just as I thought I was home free, upon my reassessment a nurse gingerly approached me and said I am so sorry, but you could possibly be in here for 6 months with rehab as you have 22 blood clots in your brain and we will need to monitor you even more closely as you could have a stroke at any moment.

I did not come this far to have a setback like this I thought. I once again immediately closed my eyes in prayer and throughout the night I envisioned busting up those blood clots like a spaceship in a Star Wars movie and prayed nonstop for a healthy brain with no issues envisioning the perfect outcome.

The next day, following up from my tests, the nurse jetted into my room and said "I don't know what you did, but you have no blood clots at all", you can be released tomorrow! I wept in relief. I'm going home.

The next day when I woke up, my mother was waiting nearby with a beautiful smile.

Then Dan came in, excited. "Just spoke to Presley. They won the championship! Presley won most valuable player! With all that kid is going through, he managed to beat his personal record for stopping shots on goal. How do you like that?"

I thought my heart would burst with happiness.

All the Things You Need to Live For

There's plenty of time to think in the hospital, especially on the healing side of a brush with death. You think of what you need to live for and it is clearly defined of what's important and what's not.

The stars aligned to grant me what only few achieve: a successful recovery and a bonus life. My Dad was right. I was going to be okay. I considered those words daily, my heart humming with gratitude for God's grace.

I reflected on a life punctuated by hard times and bitter disappointments – loss, depression, deceit, lies and heartbreak.

The most devastating heartbreak was Presley's father. Hopelessly smitten with each other, we dated, then moved in together with plans to marry. We were both overjoyed when I became pregnant with Presley. All was perfect in our world, until suddenly it wasn't. With no explanation for his change of heart, the love of my life became sullen and withdrawn, leaving me hurt, lonely, confused.

I was devastated to learn he had another secret family and after breaking my heart, he locked both me and Presley out of the home with no food or diapers at a tender age of 8 weeks old. He said he never told me because he didn't want us to leave. Unfathomable.

After a long, expensive court battle, the greatest sadness is he chose to never show up and share any of Presley's life. But after divine intervention, all personal papers were lost and Presley reclaimed his Lester name and we became an unstoppable team filled with joy. A prayer answered and the greatest joy of my life is being Presley's mom.

There were other challenges and sacrifices: giving up a job I loved to help my Father run the family business after his brother and business partner died unexpectedly. What was meant as a temporary detour on my music career path became permanent. Then a fire burnt the 40 year old family business to the ground.

As for losses, my Father's death was one of the most profoundly sorrowful experiences in my life. After he was diagnosed with pulmonary fibrosis I spent many days at his hospital bedside, holding his hand, sometimes singing.

One conversation will stay with me forever. Dad knew he didn't have much time left and was afraid to die. He needed spiritual comfort and sought my guidance with prayer and so I wrote him a personal singing prayer song for him to sing with called "Faith". Him finding peace with God was his final gift to me. His last words to me were "Happy Birthday Love - you go sing".

These experiences have all been steps in my journey to spirituality. Learning what it means to have faith is accepting that sometimes God has to bring you to your knees to make you look up.

I've also had many blessings. A happy carefree childhood. The joy of motherhood.

Family and friends who truly love me. And the pursuit of my music – a deeply fulfilling endeavour.

I've developed an ever-deepening understanding of faith and appreciation for everyday miracles – both big and small. If we take the time to look, angels are near at every turn. I can say with certainty that during my near-death experience, they were watching over me every step of the way. My takeaway? We are only one breath away from losing it all or becoming who we are meant to be. Treasure every day, for in a single breath everything can change.

## ABOUT THE AUTHOR

# LISA LESTER

SCAN TO KNOW MORE

*Singer, songwriter and entrepreneur extraordinaire, Lisa Lester has a voice that can touch your heart –bringing you to tears in one moment,making your heart sing the next. Beyond her music, Lisa now shares her life's journey in a stirring memoir - One Breath Away. Similar to one of her top Nashville recorded singles- I Have Arrived - the book hits all the right notes, setting the tone for an incredible story of survival through a life fraught with setbacks, including a miraculous recovery from a near death experience. It speaks of overcoming adversity when life was less than kind, chronicling her journey through the pivotal experiences that shaped her ever-deepening spirituality.*

CHAPTER

# 6

# One Day At A Time

LAUREN CHRAPOWITZKY

When I was eleven years old, it was the very first time I wanted to end my life. I grew up always being teased by the other kids at school. One day, after being picked on while coming home on the bus, I took a knife from the kitchen and went downstairs to the basement, where I was ready to end it all. I knew my grandmother, who had recently passed away at the time, would not have been happy to see me do this—nor would my parents, who would have been the ones to find me in the basement when they got home from work. It was the first time I cried, wiped my tears away, dragged myself back up the stairs, and put the knife back in the drawer. I buried the pain, and all I could do was tell my mom that this particular group of kids had picked on me. To this day, my parents never found out I tried to end my life that day.

When I was twenty-eight, I can remember it just like it was yesterday—waking up every morning with the heaviness of all my depression. It felt like I was hit with a blow to my chest. Some days, getting out of bed to take a shower was the only thing I would be able to accomplish for that day, and the rest of the day I would sleep. When I was asleep, the dreams would come to torment me even more. One of the dreams I had was of a black figure chasing me in a cemetery. The next dream I had was when I was locked in a gray storage room with other women barely wearing any clothes, with bunk beds everywhere. Then two huge 90s troll doll figures came into the room with guns, threatening us, and all I wanted to do was protect the other women, but I didn't know how I could save them. I remember waking up calling out for my mother, and I just couldn't go back to sleep that night. I was so scared to see what would happen next when I closed my eyes. I once told a friend who is a therapist about my dreams, and he said I was all the women who I wanted to save. It was the start of me developing issues with anxiety. I felt I had a huge heavy rock sitting on my chest that wouldn't go away.

My darkest hour lasted a year for me. Every day I would wake up and try to go about my day, and I would end up thinking of ways to kill myself. Some days I would get an urge as I was driving—what if I drove my car into a tree at full speed? Other days I thought that I should take multiple pills at once, or I could take a knife and just end my life. I would drink sometimes until I fell asleep because it was easier to fall asleep when I was intoxicated. I didn't have to think about all the pain I was consistently in. I felt like I was living with the barrel of a gun pointing against my forehead. I was living in complete darkness, and all I could see was blackness. I felt I was walking around not able to see anything, even though it was daylight outside. I would pray that it would all end somehow—all the darkness just to be taken away so I would be able to get better. I just kept thinking, "Let me get through this day today." That was all I needed at that moment.

When I finished getting my bachelor's degree, I needed to find a job. I took the first opportunity that came my way and started working for Starbucks in my hometown. Going to work was the only thing that helped me get out of bed. It was a moment where I was distracted and didn't always think about all the pain I was feeling. Working gave me a reason to get up and get out of bed when all I wanted to do was not exist. I kept telling myself all I had to do was get through today. That small sentence was my saving grace. "Just get through today, one day at a time" was all I needed to keep me going. I still use it today when things get really hard again for me.

I stayed working for Starbucks for five and a half years. It wasn't always an easy job, but I learned management skills and continued to work on customer service skills. I met a few great customers along the way who helped me keep going when things got rough. Some became good friends, and I would be able to confide in them about the difficulty I was facing at the time. At the end of my Starbucks career, I lost two important friendships that meant so much to me. At the time I was devastated, but I slowly learned: if these two people didn't care, then why should I? I slowly moved on from them and haven't looked back. When I do, I know I'm better off without them. I realized I didn't need people who didn't care about me, even though I was always there when they needed me.

I got to a point where I felt that I needed something better to do with my life, so I told my parents that I needed to quit all the jobs I was working to look for something that I was searching for to do with my life. I ended up working for a small coffee shop and Home Depot as part-time jobs temporarily until I found what I was looking for. The coffee shop was in a hospital, and at one point they shot a movie there. I met Dustin Hoffman, Ben Stiller, and Adam Sandler while they were shooting the film. They were all very nice, and in one of the scenes you can see me in the back at the coffee shop helping a customer. Sadly, I accidentally fell down the stairs to the basement in my house and broke my foot. I spent four months at home with no income coming in and nothing to do. It was a very depressing time for me—the only time I left my house was to see the doctor and go to the grocery store with my mom. By the end of my four months at home, I was able to race through the grocery store and hop over furniture like a pro. My mom wasn't too happy when I did that sort of stuff.

It was time for me to find a job after four months of trying to heal from my broken foot. I had lost so much money paying bills from what I had saved that I took whatever I could get at that moment. I started working in the cafe at Barnes & Noble, even though the doctor told me not to find work where I was standing for long periods of time, but I still took the job. It was a part-time gig, and I needed a job as fast as I could get one because the money I had was running low. I figured I could keep looking until I was able to find something else. I worked there for a whole year until I was ready to work full-time again. I applied for a full-time position but didn't get it for whatever reason the management had at Barnes & Noble where I was currently working. I had to find something else to do on top of what I was doing, or find a full-time job altogether.

At one point I was working three jobs before my accident and had no job title for any of my jobs. I started working as a teacher assistant at a daycare on top of working at Barnes & Noble. I had over $100,000 in debt from student loans and a credit card I had to pay for. I was struggling financially even though I had a somewhat better job than what I was doing before, but I was barely making any money. I wasn't even in a position to move out of my parents' house. I loved working with the kids but felt I was missing something from what I needed to be doing with my life. I felt lost, stressed out all the time, and emotionally drained from my daily life. I needed to try to find something else that would help me move forward in my life.

I ended up going to another daycare in my hometown. I felt like I was making somewhat of a difference by helping these underprivileged kids who didn't have much. I would send home boxes of cereal, what was left over from that day's snack, or whatever else I was able to find in the kitchen to give to whoever needed food that night to eat. My particular classroom was involved in a situation with a student who was hit with a belt at one point. It was difficult to see these kids in different situations of hard times that they were living in. I was lucky that I had never had to experience some of the sad situations growing up that these kids experience every day, but still, I learned a lot from them. The majority of the kids were of Hispanic background. I would sit with them and ask them, "What does this mean in your language?" and "How do you say certain words?" so I could learn to talk to them—especially to the kids who were barely able to communicate with me in English. Kids never fail to amaze me with the things they say and do, and I also made a lot of great friends with my coworkers I worked with at the school. Some I still keep in touch with to this day. We laughed, cried, and expressed our stress to one another in our daily lives together. It's always easier to deal with hard times when you have great people who laugh with you.

I've always enjoyed working hard and didn't mind tough jobs. I was put into a classroom where it was just that. It was me, my head teacher, and twelve mostly bilingual students. I was the one who had to make sure all the backpacks were checked every day, and any important papers and homework were sent home every day. The artwork for the kids to do was mostly created by me. If it wasn't what my head teacher wanted, I would have to recreate what I had done and do what she wanted all over again. I loved how hard I had to work every day in that class and felt I was truly helping in these kids' lives. Some of the kids were able to come to school, feel that we cared for them, and know we were there for them when they needed us. Some kids had more support when they were at school with us than when they were at home. Some of the kids came from abusive parents, surrounded by drugs and violence right in front of them daily. The following year, I was sent with my head teacher to a bigger room with more kids. After a few months, I just couldn't take the way my head teacher was treating me, and I still was barely making any money at all. I needed to continue to look for what I needed to be doing with my life. I still was struggling with ending my life from time to time, and the amount of stress I was feeling was not a good situation for me to be in. I needed to leave and find something different.

I just couldn't take the stress anymore and didn't see another way out of the situation that I was in. I went back to Barnes & Noble as a full-time barista and thought I would be able to make it somehow there in the world of coffee. I have met all kinds of different people and love the conversations that I have when I am working in that setting. At the time, the cafe was a hot mess. Items were everywhere, products were over-ordered, and the place was losing tons of money. I knew how to order what we needed for the cafe and knew that within a few orders, I would know what to order exactly to help save the cafe money. I did just that—I started saving the store tons of money with what we needed. The place was being organized, and I was constantly upselling products for the cafe. The cafe was looking good, and customers were coming in more because of all the hard work I was doing. I felt good about all my hard work. Then my manager hired a new cafe manager, and I was not happy about it. I was the one who turned the place around. I had the staff listening to me when I asked them to do things around the cafe. Now everything just became harder for me trying to do my job. I was tired of not being heard and didn't feel like doing all the work while getting walked on. I had to keep going to look for what I needed in my life. I started looking again for something else.

I still felt at times how easy it would be if I just took everything into my own hands and ended my life. I would get so tired of changing jobs every few years, starting over, and how little money I was making at the time. I still had tons of money I had to pay back to my credit card and school loans. I wasn't doing what I really wanted to do with my life anyway, and I was constantly circling the drain looking for something that would make me happy. I was drowning and felt that if I wasn't here, it all wouldn't matter anymore. It's so hard to get up every day when what you are doing isn't what you need or want to be doing. Nothing I had done before was a fulfillment to me.

I started working at my third daycare job a month before COVID. I didn't understand what was happening at first. I had just started working at my job, and I was hearing talk of everything shutting down. I had a job that would not keep me because I was a new employee, and I would have to start looking for something else to do. My job spoke to all teams separately and told us we had to clean the classroom as best as we could. We would be doing Zoom classes online a few times a week. We would have to recreate lessons and activities on our own for the kids to watch and do at home. I had a great time learning to make the videos and posting them online for the kids. Another skill I could say that I can do. I had a chance to become very creative with playing my clarinet, reading books online to the kids, creating art projects from home, and doing little science experiments all from my kitchen or outside in the backyard. The regular classes were a bit of a challenge for me because I didn't really know the songs that they sang to the kids, and I would rather just read and do the main song that we always did in the beginning of circle time.

I think the biggest challenge for me during COVID was watching all those people die. Watching the news every day from my living room was as depressing as it was going to get. I felt so sad for these people and their families. Hearing all the stories of millions of people all around the world getting the virus, in the hospitals without their loved ones with them, and all the horrible side effects that they had to deal with knowing they could die at any moment. I got to a point that I couldn't just keep sitting inside my house and watching the news every day—I was going mad and needed something to take my mind off what was happening. I could barely go to the store to get groceries without feeling stressed out with all the other people going too. I couldn't send my parents into the store—they are both older, and my father has health issues. Both were prime candidates for COVID. I had to do all the shopping and get whatever medicine my father needed from the pharmacy. I was stressed out, and so were all the employees who were working at the time in the stores. I would come home sometimes and cry because I just couldn't understand how mean everyone was. I tried to be understanding and patient when I went out to do the shopping, but it was hard to deal with everything that was happening all around me. Some days I thought it would be easier to protect my parents if I wasn't around anymore. I couldn't get the virus and give it to them if I was six feet in the ground. I felt so horrible and scared to bring the virus home even though I was doing everything that they had told us to do—stay away from others in the store and wear a mask. I just kept seeing people dying and was having a hard time worrying about giving it to my parents if I got it. I thought I could write a note to tell them what I wanted to do, where they would find my body, and go into the woods with a knife to take my life. At the same time, I knew my family needed me to be there, so I pushed the thoughts away and kept going forward by being there for them.

I started walking outside with a mask on for exercise to help with my stress and depression issues due to all the overload of people dying on the news. I had gained a lot of weight in my late twenties and early thirties. I had at that point lost a lot of the weight but still needed to lose more weight due to the fact I was thirty pounds overweight. Staying at home and stress eating was not helping me. So, Monday through Friday, after my classes online with the students, I went out for a walk. I still was having issues running because I had broken my foot a few years earlier, so I kept with the walking at that point. Once I felt better, I started weight training at home in my room again after years of not doing it at all. It helped me a lot with all my emotions that I just couldn't handle at the time.

I was allowed to go back to work after three months of staying at home due to COVID. It was not easy to go back to work—I was still so afraid of getting the virus and bringing it back home to my parents. I knew that I would at least be the one to do my part. I was lucky because my head teacher felt the same way I did about being careful and only going to the grocery stores and work. We both didn't get COVID until much later, and I did what I could to not give it to my parents.

I had a rough couple of years getting back to work after the lockdown and losing some important relationships along the way that I thought the other people involved had cared about me. I was at one point humiliated by one of them and was having a tough time understanding why someone could just be so cruel when I cared about them as much as I did. I had to see some of these people at work every day, so it was extra hard to deal with it at the time. So much so that I started to have panic attacks—it felt like I was sucking air through a straw and wasn't able to breathe. It was hard to try and calm myself down on my own. I didn't know what was happening to me at the time and didn't find out until later what it was that I was experiencing. I had learned I was having panic attacks on top of my anxiety and depression issues. At one point, I was dealing with so much from the loss of people I truly cared about and having a family member committed because they tried to commit suicide. I was sleeping one night when all of a sudden I sort of woke up, but not completely. I tried to move my body and open my eyes, but I was not able to do either. Somewhere I saw a female figure on top of me with long hair hanging down, a scary dark face on top of me holding me down as I was lying there unable to move. I wanted to scream but could not make a sound. Eventually, after trying to get up, the lady was gone and I was able to fully wake up and sit for a while. I told a friend about what had happened, and he said it was a demon named "The Old Hag" who came to visit me that night. After it was gone, I learned about the demon and sleep paralysis, which is when you are not fully asleep but try to wake up. It was a really scary experience for me at the time. I wanted to leave the job so badly to get away from the situation, but after being brought back after COVID, I thought that I owed my job a year of work before I left, so I stayed at the daycare. After getting my COVID shots during work hours, I again decided to stay another year because I owed them that much.

The very last straw for me that made me want to change my life around and do better came just over two years ago. I was scammed out of $7,000. For some people that may not be much, but for someone like me who doesn't have much money, that is a lot. I couldn't believe that it happened to me. I trusted someone that I barely knew and messed up big time. After that happened, I decided that it was most important to pay all that money back as fast as I could. I paid my credit card company $500 a month, made sure I was still able to pay all my other bills on time on top of that, and stopped buying anything that I really didn't need. Anytime my job asked me to work overtime, I took it and used the extra money on top of the $500 to pay off my credit card. As long as I had money for gas to get to work and money to get coffee a few times a week, I was alright. It was hard walking around all the time with the weight of what I had done to myself and how stupid I was. If only I had told someone sooner what was happening, then I would not have lost as much or any at all. I hated social media and had all my accounts locked down. I blocked whoever looked suspicious or I just didn't trust. I changed my email and my phone number and had to change all my account information to be on the safe side in case they were able to find that information out. I kept an extra watch on all my money going in and out. It was a true living nightmare. I only confided in certain people because I didn't want all of it to get out that this had happened to me. I felt so ashamed and embarrassed by what I had done.

I made a careful list of how much each bill would be and what it would cost for me to take care of this problem as soon as possible. Not only did I pay back the money I was scammed out of on one of my credit cards, I also paid off my other credit card that had money on it, and I also took care of my outstanding balance to my student loans almost a year ago. I paid back any money I owed my parents that they had loaned me. I was able to make things right finally. What had happened had not only made me want to be a better person to other people because of what I went through, but also to myself. I owed myself the love that I never got from other people I wanted in my life. It was my hardest lesson that led me to change my life around for the better.

One of the things that always helped me get through the hard times was music. I started playing the clarinet when I was ten years old. My first year of playing the clarinet, I didn't care too much and wouldn't practice, but something in me changed going into my second year of playing. Music and the clarinet became my best friend, as I didn't have many growing up. I would play for an hour to three hours every day. All I wanted to do was pick up my clarinet and get lost for hours and forget about everything I was going through. It helped me survive. I played music all through high school, adding the alto saxophone to my list of instruments to play. I went off to attend Berklee College of Music in Boston, Massachusetts, for a year and transferred to Manhattanville College in Purchase, New York. At Manhattanville, I added the flute and piano to the list of instruments I can play. I have to admit I'm not very good at the piano, but I needed the credit to graduate at the time. I worked as a music teacher for a private school in Westchester, New York, for eleven years and taught a few years privately on my own. I would love to make playing the clarinet important to me again like it once was when I was a kid. It gave me a purpose to get up every day and live for something that made me happy. I'd like to make it a profession again of mine, even if it's part-time work. I love playing music and performing, and I really miss playing music a lot. I need to focus on my passion again and make music my priority, just like fixing my finances was at the time.

I still don't have it all figured out yet—where my life is heading—but I am working hard trying to take care of myself and mend what I have lost along the way. I am trying to get back to the person who I once was, who enjoyed writing, playing music, and creating art. I am hoping that I will be able to make all my creative skills become a career move that I can earn an income from someday. I know I still have a long and hard journey ahead of me, but I would rather be on this one that will help me be the person that I always wanted to be as a child. Just being able to write all this out has helped me find a part of me I thought I had lost and needed to let out. I have felt for a while that I needed a way to tell my story, as hard as it is to tell it. I know it will help me grow as a person and open doors for me just by telling what I have been through. It has allowed me the confidence to know that I am heading in the right direction in my life to something much better.

## ABOUT THE AUTHOR

# LAUREN CHRAPOWITZKY

SCAN TO KNOW MORE

*Lauren Chrapowitzky is a passionate musician and lifelong learner based in New York. She began playing the clarinet at age ten, later mastering the flute, alto saxophone and the piano. She earned her Bachelor's degree in Fine Arts from Manhattanville College, performing in various ensembles along the way.*

*Beyond music, Lauren loves reading historical fiction and thrillers. She loves taking walks and hiking near her hometown. She cherishes the time she spends with family, friends and her puppy, Joey. A storyteller at heart, she believes in the power of music and personal experience to inspire and connect.*

CHAPTER

7

# From Panic and Pain to Power and Light

*My journey with Osteogenesis Imperfecta Type 4.*

RACHEL KERR

My parents were high school sweethearts. I was born in Dundee, Scotland, in 1994 - the middle child of three and the only girl. My older brother Andrew had arrived in 1992, and my younger brother Callum completed our trio in 1996.

For the first few years of my life, I was like any other child, full of energy and curiosity. I dreamed of dancing, gymnastics, and all the adventures that lay ahead. My family felt solid, united, and I believed in the safety of our world together.

But this ordinary childhood was about to be shattered.

By the time I was four, I had already suffered several fractures: my tailbone, my collarbone, and some cracked ribs. The doctors diagnosed me with arthritis, a misdiagnosis that would later prove significant. The first break I truly remember was on Millennium night at a family party. I fell and broke my femur; I was five. My leg was put in a cast and traction for weeks. It was then that doctors delivered the diagnosis that would change everything: Osteogenesis Imperfecta Type 4, a genetic condition that makes bones extremely fragile.

This was my call to adventure, though I didn't know it yet. Life was asking me to become someone I never imagined I'd need to be.

In 2001, we moved to Switzerland for my dad's work. I was excited about the adventure - it was new, and we were together, a solid family unit. My brothers and I started at the local primary school, where everyone spoke Swiss German. Before long, we were all fluent, making friends and settling in well. For a brief moment, I thought I could return to that ordinary world.

But my fractures started to increase with alarming frequency. I remember the sharp, brutal feeling of intense pain vividly. I can still hear the snaps echoing in my brain; sometimes I feel those sensations bursting through me as they did then. The image of my mum's face hovering above me each time, telling me, "It's okay, darling, it's okay," is something I'll never forget. This was the beginning of years of fractures, hospital stays, and surgeries that would define my childhood.

Bones across my body kept breaking, refused to heal properly, and would re-fracture without warning. I often needed physiotherapy and had to use a hydrotherapy pool to learn to walk again. As a child, I had boundless energy and wanted to do everything, not an ideal combination with OI. I often felt trapped within my own body, betrayed by the very framework that should have supported me.

It became clear that I had to stop doing activities that were too physically demanding, like dancing and gymnastics - pursuits I'd fallen in love with. This was my first refusal of the call; I didn't want to accept that my life would be different. I fought against the restrictions, against the reality of my condition, desperately trying to maintain my old life.

The medical team tried different approaches. They fitted me with an external fixator running from the top of my femur to my knee for several months. I always hated it because you could see the flesh around the metal pins, which I would meticulously clean with cotton buds myself - a ritual that made me feel slightly more in control of my circumstances.

The fractures continued relentlessly. I spent countless periods in casts, wheelchairs, or on crutches, often feeling deeply embarrassed by my limitations. One particularly difficult period involved a half-body cast with a strategically placed cut-out hole. I cried extensively during that time, but I was always adapting to new circumstances - a skill I didn't realise I was developing.

I learned to navigate life at surprising speed in my triangular cast, and once it was removed, my brothers and I transformed it into a racing track for our toys. People often perceived me as weak; however, whilst my bones were fragile, my spirit remained unbreakable. I was constantly pushing through pain, refusing to let my condition completely dictate my life.

When the fractures showed no signs of stopping, the medical team decided to start inserting permanent fixators and pins, a more invasive approach that marked a turning point in my treatment.

In the water, I found my first mentor - swimming itself. When I was submerged, I discovered a rare sense of freedom. The water held me, supported me, and for the first time, I felt what it was like to move without the constant fear of breaking. Swimming became my guide, teaching me that there were ways to find strength and grace despite my limitations.

Missing substantial amounts of school and time with friends became routine. I often felt profoundly left out, watching life happen around me from the sidelines. Children can be cruel, harsh words were frequently directed at me, teasing and name-calling related to my fragile bones becoming part of my daily reality.

The hospital became like a second home. I knew all the nurses by name, and my mum had a permanent bed next to mine during my frequent admissions. My mother emerged as my greatest mentor during these years, showing me resilience, teaching me that love could be constant even when everything else felt uncertain.

Primary 7 brought a pivotal moment. For the first time, I hurt myself badly but remained silent because I desperately didn't want to miss the school trip. I was recovering from a fractured leg and slipped whilst using my crutches. The pain in my thigh felt exactly like the fracture cracking again, a sensation so vivid that even now, thinking about that incident makes me feel queasy. I was so utterly exhausted by the constant cycle of injury and recovery that I chose silence over honesty.

When I began growing my adult teeth, it became apparent that my dental development was also affected by my condition. I had a metal rod inserted across the top of my gums, which I had to adjust every night with a metal key to gradually widen my jaw. Combined with braces, this treatment eventually resolved many of my dental issues, though it added another layer of medical intervention to my already complex routine.

Throughout my childhood, I underwent regular rounds of bisphosphonate treatments. These required three-day hospital admissions every other month, adding significantly to the already overwhelming amount of time I spent in medical facilities. Each treatment cycle meant more time away from normal childhood experiences, more time feeling different from my peers.

My first real threshold crossing came through pain medication. In retrospect, I believe my body became addicted to adrenaline, constantly seeking that rush of intensity. From a young age, I was given substantial amounts of morphine to manage my pain. From about eight or nine years old, the hospital allowed me to control my own morphine pump, which I could activate every seven minutes.

You can be certain I was pressing that button every seven minutes without fail. Whilst it genuinely helped with my pain, looking back as an adult, I can see that even as a child - though I didn't understand it then - I also craved the warm, fuzzy sensation that morphine provided. It offered comfort and ease in a world that felt chaotic and painful. This was my first taste of escape, my first crossing into a different realm of experience.

Of course, my body was genuinely suffering from the constant pain of fractures and surgeries, but I distinctly remember at least two incidents where I wasn't in significant pain but still requested morphine. This early relationship with pain medication would prove significant in my later struggles.

In 2003, our family welcomed another addition - my third brother, Thomas. His arrival brought tremendous joy to our household, and we were all delighted to have another sibling. Unfortunately, he was also diagnosed with OI, adding another layer of complexity to our family's medical journey.

We lived in a very small village where there were only sixteen children, all of similar ages with no more than five years separating the oldest from the youngest. In this isolated environment, myself and my friends began experimenting with things we shouldn't have been doing at our age -

exploring each other's bodies in ways that, as adults, we've discussed and recognised as somewhat common in such closed communities.

At age eleven, I encountered what would become a darker mentor - a boy who had joined our school from the care system. He introduced me to self-harm, showing me how to cut my wrists. I began experimenting with this dangerous behaviour, crossing another threshold into a world where pain could be controlled, where I could choose when and how to hurt.

I started high school with the same friendship group, and we gradually expanded our circle to include others. My friends became my chosen family - the people I could turn to when I needed to escape the mounting tension at home, where stress, arguments, and constant pressure were becoming unbearable.

My anxiety levels increased dramatically, and my mood plummeted. My behaviour began deteriorating noticeably. I returned to cutting, finding that I enjoyed the sensation, though it didn't provide the emotional release I was desperately seeking. I concealed my self-harm by wearing bracelets to cover my wrists.

My friendship group became my allies in rebellion. We moved on to shoplifting, primarily makeup and small items. We continued until we were caught and grew bored of the thrill. Always seeking the next excitement, we discovered boys and alcohol.

My first experience with being drunk occurred when I was twelve years old. The sensation was revelatory. I felt genuinely good, liberated even. I loved everything about it. That moment marked the discovery of what would become my primary vice for years to come.

When I drank, my body seemed to go numb. The chronic pain I was beginning to experience from years of fractures and surgeries would quiet down, whilst my head rushed with euphoria and my body felt truly free for the first time. It was intoxicating in every sense of the word.

My friends became my entire world. We smoked cannabis regularly and drank whenever possible. I'd invariably drink to excess, but we also spent considerable time simply being together, finding solace in our shared experiences. However, my behaviour was becoming increasingly reckless. I found myself in various forms of trouble and eventually had to complete community service at age fourteen after being involved in a police car chase.

But I was also encountering enemies - people who judged me, teased me, made me feel lesser than. My condition made me a target, and I was learning to armour myself with substances and rebellion.

Multiple factors influenced my parents' decision to move back to Scotland, but regardless of their reasons, the decision was made and the countdown began. This felt like approaching the inmost cave, leaving everything familiar behind, facing the unknown.

I spent every possible moment with my friends, knowing our time was limited. They created numerous keepsakes for me - books and boxes filled with memories of our shared experiences. When the time came to leave, my mother literally had to pry my fingers away from my friends as we clung to each other desperately.

Scotland didn't feel like home to me then - Switzerland was where I belonged. I was furious with my parents at the time, though I understand their reasoning now. We moved to a small town in Scotland called Dunblane, and I started school there a few months before my fifteenth birthday.

This move represented my approach to the inmost cave - the deepest, darkest place where I would have to face my greatest fears about identity and belonging. Within a remarkably short time, I had made new friends and was being invited to social gatherings and having people over to my house.

Without any conscious planning, I made a pivotal decision upon moving to Dunblane: I would completely deny my Osteogenesis Imperfecta. I told absolutely no one about my condition. This was my entry into the cave - the place where I would lose myself completely in lies and deception.

Fortunately, my fractures had slowed down, a common pattern with OI Type 4, so I could pass off occasional breaks as clumsiness or simply bad luck. Though some people might have learned about my condition through my brothers, I consistently denied it, deeply embarrassed by what I saw as a weakness.

This denial felt liberating initially, but it also meant I was living a lie that required constant vigilance to maintain. I began drinking most weekends, finding that alcohol provided the escape I craved from the complexities of my life.

I moved between different friendship groups until I found one particular circle that felt right. Our daily routine consisted of attending school - when we could be bothered - sitting around the local park, drinking, smoking cannabis, and taking whatever substances we could get our hands on.

Initially, I was participating at the same level as everyone else. However, I had developed a special relationship with alcohol that went beyond casual experimentation. It made me feel invincible and safe simultaneously. Alcohol was becoming my crutch, my most reliable friend in an unreliable world.

My drinking habits became increasingly regular. By age sixteen, I was often having whisky or whatever alcohol I could access before school to help me get through the day. At weekends, we would persuade adults to buy us bottles, and my consumption continued to escalate.

I also began engaging in sexual activity more frequently. There was one particular boy in our friendship group - popular and charismatic - who seemed to have an inexplicable hold over me. He would tease me publicly but privately invite me to his house for secret encounters. We had sex several times, though he would often mock me for my weight in front of others, as would several people in our group.

My drinking was spiralling completely out of control. I had multiple incidents requiring medical intervention - stomach pumping, losing consciousness, injuring myself whilst intoxicated, and being picked up by police. Each incident was more serious than the last, yet I seemed unable to stop the destructive pattern.

Then came the night that changed everything. I struggle to reconstruct it fully, even now. My memories of that night exist only in fragments, split-second images that I've tried countless times to piece together into a coherent narrative.

I remember sneaking to the back door of the house, stumbling badly. The memory lasts only a millisecond. I can see Grease Boy standing there wearing his distinctive knitted frog hat - an image that still triggers me when I see similar hats. Again, it's only a moment-long memory, but crystal clear.

I remember stumbling into the wall on my way back to my room, my vision severely blurred. The next memory I have is of noise surrounding me - my phone ringing insistently, someone banging on my door, my dad shouting. I realised my bedroom window had been opened fully, which was unusual.

My phone kept ringing, so I forced myself to answer it. The caller was a friend from our group. "Do you know what just happened, Rachel?" Her tone was strange, as though she had gossip to share. I don't think she truly understood the gravity of what she was about to tell me.

She explained that Grease Boy had telephoned her and told her he had sex with me whilst I was unconscious, then jumped out of my window when my father started banging on my locked bedroom door. I hung up immediately.

This was my ordeal - the moment I faced death of my innocence, my sense of safety, my ability to trust. I got dressed and walked out the back door without even taking any alcohol, as I still felt drunk. At sixteen, I couldn't fully comprehend what had just happened to me.

I walked down the hill from my house and along Dunblane High Street, experiencing waves of nausea. I was already making excuses in my mind: "It's okay, that wasn't rape," I told myself. "You've slept together many times before with your consent, so what he did wasn't wrong." I sat on the bench at the bottom of Dunblane High Street until a guy from our friendship group found me.

He asked if I was okay and seemed to believe something terrible had just occurred. He was calling it rape - a word I wasn't ready to hear. The information spread rapidly, first through our friendship group, then throughout much of the school.

Someone wrote "Grease Boy is a rapist" on the wall of the local shop where everyone congregated, which I hated seeing. However, I continued to blame myself entirely. "This is all my fault," I would think repeatedly. It took considerable time, counselling, and conversations with trusted adults for me to understand that I had been raped that night.

But from this ordeal, I seized my sword - a dark kind of power. I discovered that I could control my pain, my body, my experience through substances and self-harm. The reward was twisted but felt real: ultimate control through self-destruction.

Drinking became a daily necessity rather than a weekend activity. I was completely infatuated with alcohol and its effects. My life had never felt like it was truly in my control. First, I had been at the mercy of doctors, surgeons, and medical researchers - my body constantly being examined and operated on, my private parts regularly exposed and cleaned by others.

Then, as a teenager, I was drowning in insecurity, feeling perpetually out of place and desperate to fit in somewhere. I needed something more powerful than alcohol to feel in control of my circumstances.

I don't remember exactly how it started, but one day after eating, I put my fingers down my throat and vomited. A rush of control flooded through me; it was intoxicating. I had discovered the perfect combination of vices to help me survive my final year and a half of high school: alcohol, bulimia, sexual encounters, and prescription pain medication.

I would take my own painkillers or steal my older brother's, crushing the pills into powder in my school notebooks, snorting lines, or rubbing the powder into my gums. I fell asleep during classes more than once, was expelled from the Christmas dance for my behaviour, and barely attended lessons. I had completely stopped caring about my future or any long-term consequences.

My bulimia spiralled completely out of control. I would hide black bags filled with vomit under my bed, disposing of them at the end of each day. The secrecy and shame were overwhelming, but the sense of control was addictive.

A few months before my seventeenth birthday, I had experienced my first seizure. During this period, my relationship with my mother was severely strained. We had always been incredibly close - she had been my primary carer throughout my entire life - but I was pushing her away, lashing out at her, and refusing to listen to her concerns.

I lost weight rapidly and dramatically. I went down to a size 4, which felt like an achievement rather than a cause for concern. When I was seventeen, I attended a Halloween party wearing my little brother's army costume. He was seven years old, and the costume fit around my waist perfectly. I felt proud of this fact rather than worried about what it indicated about my health.

At eighteen, I started college and moved into my own flat in Glasgow. This represented my first attempt at the road back, trying to build a normal life despite carrying all my trauma and addictions with me.

Most nights in Glasgow, I was out drinking and engaging in casual sexual encounters, not particularly challenging when you're five feet tall with bleached blonde hair, bright blue eyes, and an outgoing personality that masked deep trauma. My bulimia began to slow down during this period, though I never sought professional help for it.

Some nights, I found myself in pleasant environments with decent people; other nights, I was sitting on the floor of empty rooms, surrounded by people who were completely intoxicated on various substances. I'm grateful that I never tried heroin, though I was offered it on multiple occasions. The closest I came to hard drugs was smoking crack cocaine.

The desperation I felt when I didn't have access to alcohol was becoming increasingly intense. I would steal, sell my possessions, or use any money I could find to buy alcohol. I would invite men over for sexual encounters as long as they brought alcohol with them. Alcohol had become like water to me, essential for survival.

I settled into Glasgow life, attending college and working various jobs, but my drinking was escalating to dangerous levels. My flatmate would regularly find me unconscious on the floor or sofa, surrounded by empty bottles. I would occasionally return to Dunblane to visit family.

During this time, another brother was born - Lewis - when I was eighteen, bringing our family to five children total.

Starting college and moving to Glasgow represented an opportunity for me to be honest about my OI, but I wasn't ready for that level of vulnerability. I remained deeply ashamed of my condition and continued to deny its existence. I carried a bottle with me constantly, always keeping a 70cl bottle of Glen's vodka in my handbag, even at college and work.

When I was nineteen, I met Peter, who would become my husband. We met at a house party one evening, and there was an immediate connection. Something about him had a calming effect on me; he was different from other men I'd encountered. His eyes seemed to communicate directly with my soul. He was the first person in Scotland to whom I opened up about my OI after keeping it secret for five years.

My drinking continued to worsen despite this new relationship. Seizures were occurring every other day, either from consuming too much alcohol or from withdrawal symptoms. Peter stood by me throughout these episodes, showing a loyalty I had never experienced before. Somehow,

I was still managing to maintain some semblance of a normal life and hold down employment.

Just before turning twenty, I suffered my worst injury yet. I fractured my spine and crushed a vertebra whilst having a seizure on a rollercoaster in Texas. Unfortunately, the metal framework inserted into my back during the emergency surgery was too large for my petite frame, and this began five years of medical hell.

Five years of misdiagnosis followed, during which I was called degrading names like "bed waster," "attention seeker," and someone who was "just there for the drugs." My local hospital already had a poor reputation, but there was severe misconduct in how I was treated during this period.

Medical staff were dismissive and refused to listen to my explanations about my own condition. I overheard nurses gossiping about me in corridors and making rude, snide remarks at my bedside. They seemed unable to separate my addiction issues from my legitimate medical condition, treating me as though my pain was fabricated or exaggerated.

For five years, I was repeatedly visiting A&E because some days I couldn't walk due to the pain. They would take X-rays, claim to examine them, and send me home without proper treatment. After enduring countless waiting lists and referrals, I finally managed to see a specialist in Edinburgh.

He took one look at the exact same X-rays my local hospital had been reviewing and immediately explained that my fracture from Texas had never healed properly; my back was still broken. My vertebra was more severely crushed than before, the metalwork was far too large for my frame and should never have been inserted, it was digging into my shoulder blades, and there were three additional stress fractures from the pressure: one at the bottom of my spine and two at the very top of my neck.

He said he would operate immediately, explaining that all I needed in my back were a few small screws. I walked out of that consultation room and burst into tears in the hallway - tears of joy and relief after years of being dismissed and disbelieved.

The previous five years had been the worst of my life up to that point. I had lost numerous jobs and spent most of my days in bed drinking bottles of straight vodka, remaining constantly intoxicated. Peter remained loyal throughout this period, and we married during these difficult years. I also attended Phoenix which is a rehab facility in Glasgow for four months.

2020 arrived when I was twenty-five, living in a tiny flat in Alloa with my husband and our three pets. I had managed to secure employment that worked reasonably well for my circumstances. My drinking habits remained problematic, but I was making constant efforts to improve.

Then COVID-19 hit, and lockdowns began. My mental health deteriorated rapidly. This period marked the first time in my life that I was attempting to heal from trauma by feeling emotions rather than numbing them with substances. This was my true resurrection, choosing to feel rather than escape.

I began experiencing severe flashbacks from childhood injuries and traumatic experiences from my youth. These would flash before my eyes and play out like vivid films.

Different flashbacks would occur at unpredictable times without any apparent trigger, whilst working, doing dishes, or engaging in routine activities.

I experienced flashbacks involving Grease Boy and several other incidents that I'm not ready to discuss here, as I'm still processing them emotionally. I sought professional support and was diagnosed with Complex Post-Traumatic Stress Disorder (C-PTSD). I was assigned a mental health nurse and engaged with her regularly.

Drinking binges still resulted in hospital admissions, but each time I became increasingly frustrated with myself. Why couldn't I simply stop this destructive behaviour? I recognised that I needed more comprehensive support. I began exercising regularly and returned to swimming in an effort to manage my chronic pain. I started attending local addiction support groups and engaging actively with them. Most importantly, I began being honest with my extended family and friends about the true severity of my condition.

In 2020, I began writing my story, journaling regularly, and practicing mindset work extensively. I learned to implement cognitive behavioural therapy techniques, which proved particularly effective for my situation. In 2019, I had also started my own travel business, though it remained largely inactive for the first few years.

For years, I kept attempting to achieve sobriety, only to fail repeatedly. Each relapse was more severe than the previous one, invariably ending with me in a hospital bed connected to an IV drip. Medical professionals began warning me about permanent health consequences, using frightening terms like "permanent damage" and "cirrhosis of the liver."

Then came another diagnosis - a chemical imbalance in my brain that helped explain some of my struggles with mental health and addiction. I had always harboured ambitious goals and dreams since childhood; I was simply consistently sabotaging my own progress.

In 2023, I spent considerable time solo travelling as part of my healing process. I also travelled with Peter, rediscovering our connection outside the context of my addiction. I began embracing activities I had previously abandoned, including dancing, yoga, and Pilates. My body became significantly stronger and more physically capable.

There were still relapses during this period. In 2023, I discovered there had been a warrant for my arrest for two years, which resulted in another night in custody. I voluntarily turned myself in, as the warrant was simply for missing a court appearance two years previously. This experience reinforced my determination: "Never again."

I continued engaging with all my support groups and mindset practices. At age twenty-eight, I was able to discontinue my anti-anxiety medication after approximately eight years of dependence. My relationship with Peter continued to strengthen as we learned more about each other and grew together.

This year has been transformative - my return to the ordinary world, but as a changed person carrying the elixir of my hard-won wisdom. I have invested considerable energy into business development, hosting my first group trips and retreats for my travel business. I've also been conducting mindset coaching calls whilst building communities in both travel and lifestyle sectors.

I've passed my driving test and recently celebrated nineteen months of sobriety - a milestone I never thought possible. I'm currently finishing my book with hopes of publishing it next year, sharing my complete story with the world. This book is my elixir, the medicine I can offer to others who are struggling with similar challenges.

I've also begun modelling and influencing, exploring creative outlets that were previously impossible due to my unstable lifestyle. We are currently undergoing Preimplantation Genetic Testing (PGT) to ensure we can have a healthy baby who won't carry my genetic condition. This has been a lengthy process spanning several years.

I feel that I'm becoming truly free and genuinely happy for the first time in my life. I remain a work in progress, but I'm more in control of my pain, my body, and my mind than I have ever been. I turned thirty last year, and I genuinely feel that my story is just beginning.

As I was writing this chapter, my brother-in-law tragically lost his life at age twenty-nine. We had bonded significantly over our shared struggles with mental health in recent years. He will be sadly and deeply missed by everyone who knew him.

We will make you proud, Kiddo. Forever twenty-nine.

The hero's journey never truly ends; it simply prepares us for the next adventure, armed with the wisdom we've gained from our trials. I've returned to the ordinary world, but I'm no longer the same person who began this journey. I carry with me the elixir of hope, the knowledge that transformation is possible, and the strength to help others find their own path from pain to power.

## ABOUT THE AUTHOR

# RACHEL KERR

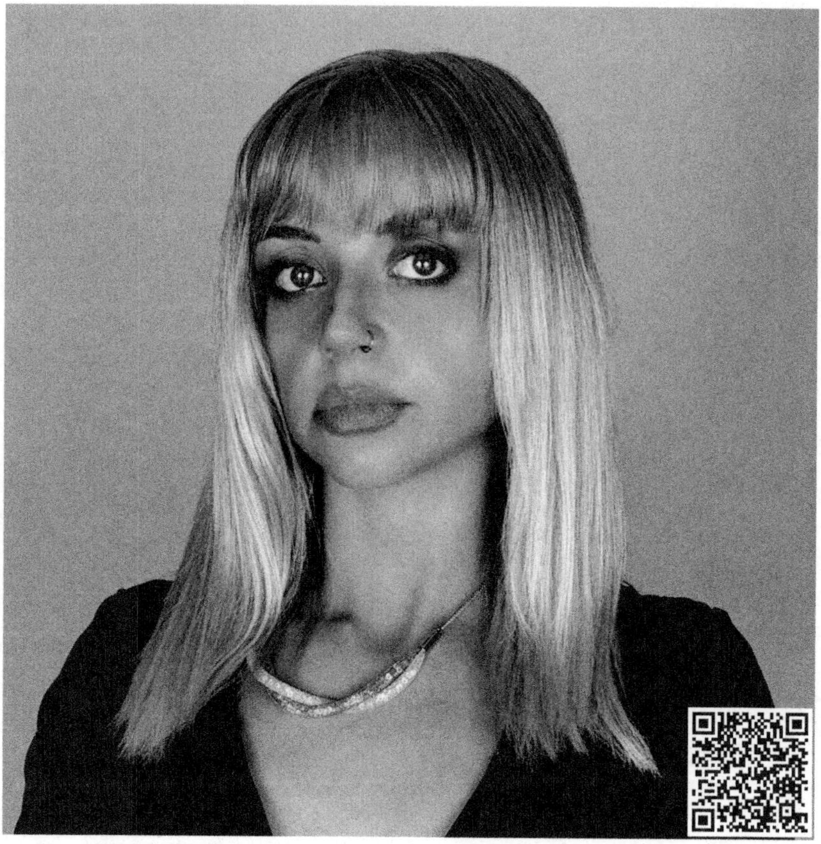

SCAN TO KNOW MORE

*Rachel's journey exemplifies the hero's path from victim to victor. Born with Type 4 Osteogenesis Imperfecta, she endured trauma, addiction, and despair before choosing transformation over destruction. Now 30 and 19 months sober, she's a coach, entrepreneur, and advocate who helps others break free from limitation. Through her travel business, mindset coaching, and storytelling, Rachel proves that our greatest struggles become our greatest strengths, and that every ending is actually a new beginning.*

START OVER VOL 4

CHAPTER

# 8

## Resilient Foundations

*A Journey of Reinvention through Property and Neurodiversity*

SHIRLEYANN HAIG

They called me "Pizza Face" because of my acne, and the bullies had a field day with my mullet. Growing up in 1980s Liverpool wasn't exactly a walk in the park. There was no silver spoon in our house - no early promise of success. I begged my mum for a shell suit like all my mates had, but instead got handed a flowery puffball dress that made my fat knees look even worse. I dreamed of Nike trainers, but all we could stretch to were "Nicks" - those knock-off versions that fooled no one.

Surrounded by scarcity and negativity, I spent my days dreaming of a life where I could buy what I wanted without checking my purse first. But despite all the challenges, my childhood held pockets of pure magic. Rain or shine, I'd be out there - walking, cycling, catching buses away from the council estate to explore parks, woodlands, beaches, and lakes. There was proper joy in those simple moments that money couldn't touch, and that perspective still shapes who I am today.

From early on, I knew I wanted more than what our council estate could offer, even if I hadn't a clue how I'd get there. My parents married young, but Dad's wandering eye split them up quick smart. Mum was just 21, a single mother with no formal education, struggling with mental health whilst on benefits. I didn't see my dad at all during primary school - not once.

To survive, we moved in with my grandparents, who became my real carers. My nan was my absolute rock, giving me the unconditional love and stability I craved. Mum felt more like a big sister than a mother.

Our family was complicated - I was the eldest of loads of half-siblings from both sides. When I met my dad again at 12, I could see why Mum always said I was like him. We had the same confident personality, same mannerisms - a perfect example of nature versus nurture. But our reunion was short-lived. Every weekend visit meant babysitting my little sister whilst he went out drinking. I grew tired of that arrangement and eventually stopped going. Despite knowing where I lived and having my phone number, he stayed out of contact for another twelve years.

Throughout it all, my nan's love never wavered. Looking back, I realise these experiences left me with deep abandonment issues that I still work through every day.

At school, I was a proper chatterbox - teachers constantly told me off for talking. I was always in trouble, had no filter, couldn't keep a secret to save my life. I craved attention and excitement, desperate to fit in, but money was always tight. So I found other ways to get what I wanted.

I turned to stealing - started with sweets from local shops and escalated to bigger things. My wake-up call came in my teens when I got arrested for shoplifting in a department store. Sitting in that cell, having my fingerprints and mugshot taken, something clicked. That day changed everything and reinforced the importance of consequences.

Education wasn't valued in our house. Mum hadn't attended school because she'd been caring for my nan who had epilepsy, so she couldn't see the point of it all. My high school had a terrible academic record, but they received funding from the Prince's Trust to create an after-school homework club.

My predicted grades were awful, but for the first time, I had academic support from people who believed in me. I had to lie to my mum, saying I was in detention, just so I could stay and study. With the staff's help, I caught up on coursework and prepared for exams. I became one of the school's highest achievers, proving to myself that with the right attitude and support, I could succeed.

At 16, the Prince's Trust invited me to travel around the UK as their "success story," speaking on big stages in major cities to headteachers, showing how programmes like ours could change lives. This experience helped me realise that my love of talking was actually a superpower in the right environment. My passion for public speaking was born.

Thousands of schools eventually implemented after-school clubs like ours, helping children like me get the support they needed. One of my proudest moments was watching 'The Crown' when Prince Charles mentioned these clubs were one of his greatest achievements. Although it was a drama series based on true events, knowing I'd been the "poster girl" for that campaign made me dead proud.

Despite studying for A-levels and completing an Art Foundation course, I was expected to contribute to household bills. I worked full-time evenings and weekends at a local hotel - demanding hours that gave me invaluable experience handling money and responsibility.

When I moved to Portsmouth to study Illustration at university, I brought that work ethic with me. I quickly rose to supervisor at the student union bar, managing a team whilst balancing studies. I thrived under pressure, and those long hours taught me resilience and time management skills that would serve me well.

An 80-hour week wasn't enough for me. Driven by a desire to challenge myself further, I joined the Territorial Army. I embraced the intense training, and my dedication paid off with several awards during the passing out parade. That period tested my tenacity and determination like nothing else, igniting a passion for pushing beyond my limits.

Even holidays were busy - each summer and Easter, I took jobs selling aerial photographs across the UK, breaking company records with door-to-door sales. I worked my way up from salesperson to area manager whilst still at university. I discovered that my natural curiosity about people and love of conversation were gifts in the sales field. I realised I had a unique skill for connecting with others - something that would prove invaluable throughout my career and life.

In 1997, during university, I met my partner. We married in 2007 after a decade together.

After university, I focused on building a career that would provide stability, financial security, and work-life balance. I took various sales roles, rising quickly and earning numerous awards. Yet despite the success, I felt unfulfilled, searching for something more impactful.

I tried temporary work in different industries to explore options. A week in a pharmaceutical company was all it took - I was hooked on clinical research and training. True to form, I enrolled in distance learning for a Postgraduate Diploma in

Clinical Research and Pharmacology whilst working. This qualification solidified my expertise, and before long, I was moving up the ladder, excelling in pharmaceutical roles.

Year after year, I found myself on stage winning company and national industry awards as top UK salesperson and coach. The high salary and bonuses allowed me a lifestyle many would envy, but whilst my friends spent money on designer clothes and luxury items, I understood money's fragility and saved instead. My frugal habits built a financial cushion - I knew I wanted my money working for me long-term.

Around this time, both my grandparents passed away, and Mum was widowed just a year after remarrying. This period affected me profoundly. I looked strong on the outside but felt incredibly sad and vulnerable, suffering terribly with IBS. My mind tried to stay strong, but my body reminded me daily of the consequences of burying emotions.

After losing the most loving person in my life, I found myself focusing on retirement and what my last years would look like. I was even more determined to create passive income for security, and realised how quickly life passes - I wanted to make a difference, leave a legacy, create financial security for everyone around me.

The turning point came when a friend introduced me to 'Rich Dad Poor Dad' by Robert Kiyosaki. That book shifted my perspective entirely, presenting concepts like assets, passive income, and financial independence. I realised that although I was doing well career-wise, I was essentially trading time for money. I wanted something more sustainable that would build wealth independent of my day job.

Inspired, I signed up for a property investment training course, eager to learn skills that could create passive income and build capital in real estate. My research showed Liverpool's property market had both affordability and potential for high returns. Ironically, my analysis led me back to the very council estate I'd once wanted to escape. Now I saw it as a valuable investment opportunity.

My parents reunited around the same time, and the area's familiarity made it a natural choice. I was living three hours away, but we made the journey every weekend for a whole year, prioritising this over everything fun our peers were doing.

In 2007, my career and personal life hit significant milestones. I married my partner of ten years, and hard work in pharmaceuticals brought substantial bonuses. Whilst the credit crunch led many to offload properties, I saw opportunity.

I took the leap and bought my first buy-to-let in Liverpool - a house in desperate need of refurbishment. Standing there looking at this run-down, boarded-up place covered in dust and paint, I questioned my choices. I was cold, tired, and regularly felt jealous of friends out partying, spending their money instead of investing it. Delayed gratification was the hard option.

I felt alternating surges of pride, confidence, and excitement, followed by fear and imposter syndrome, worrying that childhood friends and neighbours would judge me, thinking

I thought I was better than them. I fought the negative emotions and remained hands-on, managing work and learning everything about property renovations.

The experience was empowering. I quickly realised the potential of transforming neglected properties into valuable homes. Each successful renovation fuelled my ambition to expand, and I reinvested my pharmaceutical salary, bonuses, and rental income into more properties. Many childhood friends and neighbours became my tenants, and I felt proper pride offering long-term, affordable housing to people who couldn't get properties through the local council.

Using savings, I bought more and more repossessed, derelict properties across Liverpool. I poured energy into revitalising the area, transforming forgotten streets into attractive places to live. By renovating and revaluing properties, I could remortgage and recycle funds, expanding my portfolio. I even sold our own home and moved into rented accommodation to release more investment money.

Within five years, we'd acquired 17 buy-to-let properties, generating passive income that exceeded expectations. When my husband was made redundant for the second time in three years, proving corporate unpredictability, he focused on managing our business whilst I continued thriving in pharmaceuticals. The combination of my salary and property income gave us security to live comfortably and plan for our family's future.

With financial stability in place, we started our family in 2010, welcoming two beautiful boys just 18 months apart. We relocated to Wirral and moved into our dream home - a beautiful detached house with views over the River Dee and Welsh hills. I couldn't have been happier; I had everything I'd ever dreamed of and was living my best life with loads of disposable income.

In their early years, the boys were happy and easy-going. We felt incredibly lucky. But as our eldest reached school age, we noticed challenges beyond typical childhood struggles. His anxiety skyrocketed. Everyday tasks became battles - massive meltdowns, smashing his room and anything within reach. He struggled with direction, feared the unknown, and would shut down completely in unfamiliar places or around new people.

As he entered school, things grew harder. We received regular complaints from teachers about his behaviour towards staff and students. We desperately sought help but felt lost in uncertainty. With support from the PDA Society, we finally uncovered the root: he was autistic with a PDA (Pathological Demand Avoidance) profile. Understanding was a relief, but didn't make daily life easier.

Our younger son was full of energy with his own unique personality and boundless spirit, yet he too struggled to fit within standard school settings and was diagnosed with ADHD. Both boys faced repeated exclusions - not only from school but from scouts and after-school clubs, as their needs became increasingly hard for traditional systems to accommodate.

Parenting neurodivergent children brought challenges no manual could prepare me for. It was emotionally and physically draining, balancing family and work became a daily struggle. Each exclusion felt like rejection - not just of their behaviour, but of who they were as people.

The psychological cost is one few acknowledge. It's not just juggling appointments with therapists, specialists, and schools - it's constant worry, fear you're not doing enough, and heartbreak seeing your children struggle in a society that doesn't always accept their differences.

The constant tension put inevitable strain on my marriage and career. I was facing divorce, redundancy, and permanent school exclusions on top of COVID-19 upheaval.

Within six months, my life crashed down. My marriage ended, leaving me feeling like the ground had been pulled from beneath me. The person I thought I'd grow old with was gone, and suddenly I was navigating life alone. Before I could process that loss, I lost my job - a career I'd poured my heart and soul into. COVID-19 struck, eliminating any chance of finding work in my field.

My husband moved out, leaving me in a house I adored with no stable income and two sons depending on me - each needing more support than the world seemed ready to offer. I cut back, cancelled everything non-essential, put my mortgage on interest-only, and shopped in community discount supermarkets. The only thing getting me through daily bills was passive income from rental properties I'd bought 15 years earlier, but that income had to cover two households now.

I was heartbroken about all those years of studying, sacrificing, working two jobs. I'd built a life and career I was incredibly proud of - a six-figure salary in pharmaceuticals, a beautiful home on the Wirral, strong community, and family. I'd achieved everything I'd dreamed of through sheer determination and sacrifice. But life doesn't follow a script.

I questioned if I could keep going. Should I abandon everything I'd worked for or keep pushing through whilst running on empty? Physically and mentally exhausted, I spent months torturing myself, going back and forth about whether to sell up and give up or stand up and focus on my strengths.

There's something profoundly humbling about hitting rock bottom. It strips away everything - possessions, pride, self-worth - leaving emptiness that feels endless. Yet in that emptiness, I found a flicker of strength, a reminder that I'd risen once and could rise again.

Initial steps were difficult. The weight of circumstances felt overwhelming, but I had no choice except to move forward, however small the steps. I decided to focus on what I could control and began rebuilding from that foundation.

We worked with schools, giving them help and guidance, managing to get education, health care plans, and funding both boys needed. I set up my own business, Home Property Solutions Ltd, with a mission to help others create passive income to avoid facing similar challenges. I knew the property industry well and believed I could use my experience to guide people needing financial stability in an unstable world.

Starting over wasn't easy, but gradually, efforts began bearing fruit. Home Property Solutions grew, and I helped investors buy properties and let them to people most in need.

I felt renewed purpose. Financial success was rewarding, but knowing I was making a difference in people's lives truly sustained me. I focused on supporting vulnerable groups in affordable housing, particularly single mums in similar positions to me. I also took on a young ADHD mum with an ADHD daughter who was finding work difficult due to needing flexibility - something I understood too well.

Today, I'm proud of the life I've rebuilt. My business thrives, offering real value whilst giving me flexibility to support my sons how they need. I've fostered communities and businesses that empower people, finding purpose that makes every hardship feel worthwhile.

Recently, I celebrated the one-year anniversary of Inspiring Women Wirral - an amazing inclusive community I set up to help women thrive in business. I've been actively developing multiple neuro-inclusive creative training resources through Inspiring Minds Group CIC, focused on financial literacy and entrepreneurship.

Following both my children's diagnoses, their consultant recommended I be evaluated for ADHD too. In 2024, at 47, I was formally diagnosed with ADHD (Hyperactive and Impulsive type). The diagnosis was a revelation, explaining so much about my life. Looking back, I saw patterns of fearless behaviours, successes, and equally destructive situations. The hyperactivity, impulsivity, constant need for stimulation, and unwavering need for honesty, equity, and inclusiveness had shaped my experiences in ways I was only beginning to understand.

The joy of seeing my children thrive has been indescribable. The boys I was once told wouldn't make it through school are now flourishing in high school with 100% attendance and grade A achievements. Watching them succeed against all odds has been one of the most rewarding parts of this journey.

I've been honoured with several prestigious awards, including Wirral Businesswoman of the Year bronze award, finalist in New Business of the Year for Inspiring Women, and Property Business of the Year. These nominations are testament to the power of resilience and courage - a reminder that even after losing so much, we can rebuild and flourish.

For anyone reading this, know that no matter how low you feel, no matter what you've lost, you can start over. Sometimes a second chance isn't just about survival - it's about creating a life richer and more fulfilling than you ever imagined. For me, property investment became the path to freedom, and perhaps it could be the same for others.

I've been incredibly fortunate to connect with dedicated parents, experts, educators, and policymakers as passionate as I am about advocating for neurodivergent children. Together, we've shared stories, insights, and strategies, determined to bring real change for families like ours. Our experiences and collective wisdom are forming the backbone of a book I'm working on to provide resources for other parents.

The future is bright and filled with exciting, creative flexibility that I know I need to keep my ADHD brain happy. By providing long-term affordable housing as well as training and resources in financial literacy, entrepreneurship, and neurodiversity, I'm grateful for all the highs and lows - they've shaped me and driven me to help others.

Looking back at that child they called "Pizza Face," I can see now that being different wasn't a weakness - it was my greatest strength. Every challenge, every setback, every moment of feeling like an outsider was preparing me for this moment, this mission, this opportunity to help others find their own path to resilience and success.

Keep going, because sometimes the life you're meant to live is waiting just on the other side of the storm.

## ABOUT THE AUTHOR

# SHIRLEYANN HAIG

SCAN TO KNOW MORE

***Shirleyann Haig: The Ethical Passive Income Coach***

*Shirleyann Haig is a multi-award-winning entrepreneur and advocate for ethical wealth creation. As The Ethical Passive Income Coach, she teaches individuals to build sustainable income streams, empowering them to achieve financial freedom. With over 20 years of corporate experience and a thriving property portfolio, Shirleyann has turned her own challenges, including redundancy, divorce, and parenting neurodivergent children, into a mission to help others. She founded Home Property Solutions, Inspiring Women Wirral, and Inspiring Minds Group CIC to promote financial literacy and inclusion. Shirleyann's inspiring story, practical strategies, and upcoming books make her a leading voice in ethical wealth creation.*

START OVER VOL 4

CHAPTER

9

# They Called it Trauma

*I call it fuel*

MICHELLE HOGG

It's funny how the mind clings to certain memories, gripping tight as if they're the most important stories ever told. But why is it that the painful ones - the ones that cut deep - always seem clearer than the happy ones?

I've noticed this over the years, especially when my children say, "Remember when?" Their faces light up as they relive a moment, some funny or heartwarming thing we shared, and I draw a blank. It's as if my brain misfiled the good stuff, but trauma? That's organised in high definition, crystal clear, ready to play at any moment.

One night, I was sitting with my mum, talking about one of the hardest, most life-altering experiences we went through together. She was stunned at how much I remembered, every tiny detail, as if I had just stepped back into that moment. "How do you recall it so vividly?" she asked, shaking her head. The truth is, some things etch themselves into you so deeply that no amount of time can fade them.

I was only nine when that moment rocked our family, but I'll get to that soon.

My earliest memory? I must have been around three years old, maybe younger. And yet, I can still see it as if I'm right there again. If you asked most people to remember something from that age, they'd probably laugh. "No way, that's too young." But me? It's as if time folded in on itself, replaying the scene like a film I've watched a thousand times.

I was sitting at the top of the stairs, peering through the wooden banisters, heart thudding in my tiny chest. Down below, voices rose, sharp and jagged, slicing through the air. Arguments had started creeping into the walls of our home more often, the cracks widening. I didn't understand adult problems yet.

Then I saw it.

A sudden movement, grappling hands, a desperate push, and then - thud.

I should have been in bed. They didn't know I was watching, but I was always observant, always curious, always aware of things I probably shouldn't have been. And that night, I learnt what violence looked like.

Another time, I remember banging my little fists against the glass of our bay window, watching him leave. My home - the one with the beautiful window that I secretly adored - felt suddenly colder. I call those "Christmas tree windows," the kind you see in warm, happy family homes in films. Maybe that's why I've always wanted one as an adult. Maybe I thought if I had the window, I'd have the happiness that was supposed to come with it.

But that night, the window was just glass, separating me from the one walking away.

Parents separating is a common part of life. Children don't see the weight adults carry - the struggles, the exhaustion, the things they keep hidden behind forced smiles. Back then, I didn't question it. I just knew that one day, a new man appeared in my life.

My stepfather.

At first, he was wonderful - warm, loving, playful. He stepped into the role of "dad" with ease, and just like that, I had two dads and two mums. It was our new normal. For a while, it seemed as though everything would be all right.

He used to help me with my homework, patiently guiding my little hands as I learnt to write. Back then, I was the only child in the house, and whilst he was strict, I don't remember much that felt too heavy. It was just us - a structured kind of love, but love all the same.

Then something in him changed.

It wasn't overnight, but looking back, I can pinpoint when his territorial army background started bleeding into home life - not as discipline, but as punishment. It was like a switch had flipped, and suddenly, everything I did was wrong. I was too much - too playful, too loud, too full of energy. The fun, creative little girl who made up games and even had an imaginary friend? I became an annoyance. My little sister was favoured now, and it was felt.

Dinnertime became something I dreaded. If I didn't finish every last bite, I was made to sit at the table alone whilst everyone else got up and carried on with their night. It didn't matter how full I was - I wasn't finished until the plate was empty. No slouching, no relaxing. Sit properly. Act right. I remember how cruel it felt, how it made my stomach knot even when I wasn't eating.

Then came the night that shattered everything.

I was nine years old. Too young to carry what was placed on my shoulders that night, but life doesn't ask permission before it breaks you. I still want to hug that little girl, to tell her she didn't deserve what happened, that it wasn't her fault. She's healing, even now, but every so often, she still feels fragile.

I remember walking downstairs, my bare feet padding softly against the floor, drawn by something I couldn't explain. And there he was.

My stepfather, this strong, towering man, sitting on the living room floor sobbing. His eyes were raw, swollen from crying, his body hunched over as if the weight of something unbearable had finally crushed him.

I hesitated for a moment. I had never seen him cry before. Not like this.

I walked over slowly and wrapped my little arms around him. The moment I did, his body convulsed with grief, his sobs turning into something deeper - something that didn't just sound painful, but felt painful. I could feel it, radiating from him like a physical force. I didn't know what to do, how to fix it, how to make it better. I was only nine.

So I did the only thing I could. I whispered, "It's all right, Daddy." I hugged him tighter. "Everything will be all right."

But it wasn't.

He looked at me then, his eyes glassy and desperate. "Promise me you'll look after your sister," he said, his voice trembling.

I nodded, my heart pounding. "I promise."

He repeated it, searching my face for understanding. "Promise me."

"Yes, Dad. I promise."

And then I was sent to bed.

I didn't know it at the time, but that was the last time I would ever see him.

I lay in the darkness, my mind racing. Something was wrong. I knew it was. I could still feel the sadness in his body when I hugged him. It had clung to me, heavy and suffocating. I stared at the ceiling, wondering where he had gone, why he was so sad, why the air in the house felt thick and strange.

The next day, the energy in the house had shifted into something even worse - panic, tension, the kind that makes your stomach feel weird before you even understand why.

I crept up the stairs, where the adults had gathered, listening for clues, trying to make sense of what was happening. I just needed to know Mum was all right. But when I reached the top, I saw her.

She was draped over the bathtub, sobbing, her body heaving as family members tried to console her.

I froze.

Something was very wrong.

"Did he leave us?" I whispered, but no one answered.

A heart attack. That's what they said. He had a heart attack after leaving the house that night.

But I knew they were lying.

I knew what I had seen, what I had felt in his arms when he held me. And I knew, deep down, that he hadn't just died. He had made a choice. A choice no one wanted to explain to a nine-year-old girl.

They thought they were protecting me. But the truth has a way of settling inside you, even when no one says it out loud.

And just like that, the darkness began to take hold.

I wasn't allowed to attend the funeral. They said it was better that way. But it only made it worse. Grief had nowhere to go, so it buried itself inside me.

I didn't talk about it. I just carried it.

I became quieter, more withdrawn. I spent more time in my head, trapped inside a tangled mess of thoughts and emotions I didn't know how to unpack. I told myself to just get on with it. That's what people did, right? They moved on.

But I didn't.

I just learnt how to keep it all locked away.

Until he came back.

I woke up to find him standing at the foot of my bed.

I should have been scared. But I wasn't.

He wasn't like the shadowy figures I'd imagined ghosts to be - there was no cold chill in the air, no flickering lights. He just was. Solid. Familiar. But different somehow, softer. Like the weight that had consumed him in life had been stripped away.

I didn't move. I just stared.

Then he spoke.

"I'm sorry," he said, his voice gentle, almost lighter than I remembered. "Look after your mum and your little sister."

Warmth spread through the room, like the sun rising after a long, dark night.

I didn't speak. I just felt.

And then, just as quickly as he had come, he was gone.

I lay there, staring into the darkness, my heart pounding.

For the first time since that night in the living room, I let myself cry.

And somehow, I knew - I knew that wherever he was now, he had finally found the peace he had been searching for.

I wish I could say the next stepfather was different.

And in some ways, he was. At first, things were fine - we got on well enough. But life has a way of showing me the same lesson over and over again: men either leave, or they hurt me. Or both.

One night, a drunken rage after an argument that had nothing to do with me. Before I could even register what was happening, his hands were around my throat, pinning me to the wall.

I remember the pressure. The weight of his rage. The words he spat at me, laced with venom, cutting just as deep as the grip on my neck. A television was hurled in my direction, only missing me because someone else caught it in time.

I didn't fight back. I just took it. Because by then, I had already learnt: this is what men do.

That was my reality. The story I carried with me.

By the time I hit adolescence, I had already been trained to believe my worth was measured by how others treated me. I was never short on attention - sometimes from boys my age, but just as often from grown men who should have known better.

I looked older than I was. That was always the excuse. But I was still a child.

The first time I noticed a neighbour's wandering eyes, something inside me twisted. He knew my age. He knew I was too young. And yet, the way he looked at me made my skin crawl.

It was confusing - unwanted attention that, somehow, still made me feel wanted.

Then came secondary school. That's when I mistook control for love.

He was older, and he gave me the kind of attention I thought I needed. Letters filled with sweet words, songs written just for me. It felt special. It felt like love. But love shouldn't come with rules.

There were no mobile phones back then, so he'd turn up at places unannounced, watching me, making sure he knew where I was and who I was with. He'd follow me if I was out with friends. At the time, it seemed normal. Maybe even romantic.

But when you grow up witnessing control disguised as love, you don't recognise the red flags. You think being possessed means being protected.

I was only twelve when he started grabbing me by the neck if I stepped out of line. If I drew too much attention - just by being me - he'd yank me away, whispering warnings in my ear. "You're mine. Don't forget that."

I didn't know any different. I thought love meant ownership.

Then came the night that changed everything.

It happened fast. Too fast for me to understand until it was already over.

I had said no. I had pushed him away. But he didn't stop.

He kept going.

And I lay there, frozen. Overpowered. Confused.

Afterwards, I felt off. I didn't know what to call it, what to label it. I went home, my mind racing with questions I couldn't answer. Why didn't he listen? Why did my "no" not mean anything? Did I do something wrong? Was this my fault?

Shame clung to me like a second skin.

So I stayed quiet. I told no one.

I convinced myself that this was just something that happened, that I had somehow allowed it. That it was mine to carry, mine to keep locked away.

Eventually, I broke it off. I couldn't handle the way I felt owned rather than loved.

But breaking free didn't erase what had already been done.

Then the police came.

They were making inquiries, asking questions about reports they had received. When they looked at me, I wanted to lie. I wanted to pretend I didn't know anything. That nothing had happened.

So I did.

I tried.

But my poker face didn't last long.

The weight of the truth broke me open, and before I could stop myself, I was sobbing, the words spilling out in fragments.

That's when I realised what had happened to me wasn't just wrong. It was a crime.

I wish I had never told them.

I wish I had kept my poker face going, even to my closest.

Because the next thing I knew, I was standing in a courtroom, wishing I could rewind time and make it all disappear.

But being there was pointless.

They didn't listen to me. Not really.

They asked questions that confused me, twisted my words, made it sound as though I had done something wrong. Like I needed to explain myself.

If I could reach back in time and shield that little girl, I would. I would wrap my arms around her and tell them all to fuck off.

But I couldn't.

I had to be there. Answer their questions. Feel their judgement.

And when it was over, I walked out into the hallway, my knees buckling beneath me as I crumbled to the floor.

The shame was unbearable.

People stared. Faces blurred together. And yet, I felt unseen.

Nobody told me I wasn't to blame. Nobody told me I was still whole.

We never spoke about that day again.

And that's exactly how I wanted it.

I wanted it to disappear.

Like it had never happened.

I left school at sixteen and started working as a junior in a hair salon.

It was fast-paced, full of energy, and exactly what I needed - an escape wrapped in the buzz of hairdryers, gossip, and the endless rush of clients coming and going. But hairdressers didn't just love their work. They loved to party. And the wild side of me? She was ready to come out.

It was the late '90s, early 2000s. The club scene was the place to be, and looking older than I was meant nobody questioned me slipping through the doors, drink in hand, music pulsing through my veins.

Then, one night, I was handed a little pill.

I still remember her face - the woman who gave it to me. She was older, maybe ten years my senior. Maybe she saw something in me, a restless mind searching for an escape. And she had just the solution.

Ecstasy.

And for the first time in my life, I felt free.

The weight of my past, the voices in my head, the locked-up trauma - it all melted away. They didn't call it ecstasy for nothing. Euphoria wrapped itself around me like a warm embrace, and I loved it.

I danced. I laughed. I felt light.

And after that, I wanted more.

Every weekend, I chased that high, desperate to keep hold of that fleeting feeling of weightlessness. But there was a catch. One pill didn't hit the same way twice. That first experience? That was the best it would ever be. And after that, I kept taking more - doubling up, pushing limits - just trying to feel it again.

I loved having fun but it was never just about that, it was also about shutting off my mind. About silencing the noise, the memories, the unworthiness I carried like an unwanted shadow.

I didn't want to be that girl anymore. The one who was told what to do, how to behave, who to be. I wanted to be reckless. Bad. I wanted to rewrite the story of the girl who had always been powerless.

And then, one night, I went too far.

Someone handed me liquid ecstasy at a party, and without thinking, I took it.

And everything changed.

I don't know how long I was out of it, but I remember the fear. The loss of control, the way my body and mind disconnected, floating into some abyss that I wasn't sure I'd come back from.

I scared myself.

That was the moment. The too-close moment.

And I knew - I knew it was time to stop.

No more chasing highs. No more losing myself just to feel free. Because the truth was, I wasn't free at all. I was still running.

My family never knew.

They wouldn't have suspected a thing.

Because masking things? That was my superpower.

For the first time in my life, I felt safe.

Being in love properly as an adult felt like solid ground beneath my feet. We had a house, a mortgage, jobs. We were building something real, something responsible. At nearly twenty, I felt as though I was finally doing life the way it was supposed to be done. Focused. Stable. In control.

Then, at twenty-two, I found out I was pregnant.

Unexpected, yes - but a blessing. A shift I hadn't planned for but embraced wholeheartedly. I was going to be a mum.

At first, I was excited. But as my body began to change, so did my confidence.

The weight crept on, my reflection became unfamiliar, and the whispers of insecurity grew louder. My friends didn't help. "Men stray when their partner is pregnant," they told me. "They stop finding you attractive. They go looking elsewhere."

I laughed it off, but inside, anxiety spread like poison.

Was I still beautiful? Desirable? Would he still want me?

I tried to push the thoughts away, but they sat in the back of my mind, gnawing at me, waiting for proof.

And then one day, I got the phone call.

A woman's voice on the other end of the line.

I don't even remember her words - I just remember the feeling. The way my stomach dropped. The way my heart pounded so hard it felt as though it might crack my ribs.

I knew before she even had to say it.

Everything I feared had just been handed to me, confirmed in the worst way possible.

I felt worthless.

Fat. Ugly. Disposable.

Out of control.

I pressed my hands against my swollen belly, the life growing inside me, and the tears came hard and fast, burning my skin as they fell. Then, just as quickly, anger rose in their place.

Now? In this moment when I was at my most vulnerable, my most scared, but also my happiest? I was angry and confused.

The weight of it cut through me like a knife.

I had been building a home. A future. A family. And in one phone call, it all crumbled beneath me.

And the worst part?

I was stuck.

Stuck in this situation. Stuck with an unborn child who deserved stability. Stuck feeling as though I had no power, no choice, no way to undo what had already been done.

I wanted to run.

I wanted to escape.

But this time, I wasn't just running for myself.

I had a baby growing inside me - a tiny life.

And somehow, in all the hurt, I knew this wasn't just about me anymore.

All of these traumatic events pulled me deeper into my own head.

But no one would have known.

I smiled. I laughed. I showed up. Because that's what mums do. They get on with things, even when life is hard. Even when it feels unpredictable and impossible.

I was a mum now. That was my purpose.

When I had my second child, it was another blessing. Another piece of my heart outside of my body. But life had other plans, and soon, I found myself a single parent to a nearly three-year-old and a nine-year-old.

This wasn't how it was supposed to go.

I tried. I really did. I pushed through, forcing myself to keep moving, to be strong, to hold everything together. But somewhere in the process, I lost myself.

And then we lost our home.

I packed up what little we had and moved. Then moved again. And again. Six times within eight years. It felt as though life kept throwing curveballs at me just to see if I could catch them.

And I did. Every. Single. Fucking. Time.

But one move nearly broke me.

One of the places we ended up in was a high-rise, fourteen floors up, in a building that felt as though it had been forgotten by the world. The lift was ancient - every time we stepped inside, I held my breath, praying it wouldn't get stuck between floors.

When we walked into our so-called "home," I swallowed down the lump in my throat.

There were holes in the walls. Stains on the carpet. No curtains, no blinds, nothing to shut out the harsh glare of the outside world. It felt like the kind of place people survived - not lived.

I put on a brave face, trying to make it an adventure for my daughter. But I saw it in her eyes - the same unease that was clawing at my chest.

Then she said it.

"Mummy, did bad children stay here before us? Because of the holes in the walls next to my bed?"

I broke.

That night, I cried myself to sleep. And by morning, I packed our things and left.

No child of mine was ever going to feel unsafe like that. Not whilst I had breath in my body.

It was me and my babies against the world.

I found a flat - one I chose. One that I could make into a home, with the help of income support to keep us going.

I did everything I could to make ends meet.

And then, somewhere along the way, I became a businesswoman.

I was unstoppable. Determined to show my daughters that they could do anything, even on their own. That they didn't need anyone else to save them. That they had the strength to build a life for themselves.

But success comes at a price.

And for me, it was time. Precious, irreplaceable time.

I was working so hard to build a better future for them that I missed pieces of the present. Burnout swallowed me whole, but I pushed through, convinced I was doing the right thing.

And then, one day, I saw a picture.

A simple, ordinary picture of my girls when they were younger.

And suddenly, I was there again. I could smell them, feel their tiny arms around my neck, hear their little voices calling out for me.

I wanted to jump into that photo, to wrap my arms around their younger selves and breathe them in. I still do now with every old picture memory I see.

Because that's the thing about pictures.

They don't just remind you of what was.

They remind you of what you can never get back.

Just when life started to feel good, the past had a way of creeping back in.

I had built something solid - a thriving salon business, a secure home, a new relationship. For the first time in a long time, I felt stable. Like maybe, just maybe, I had finally broken free from the cycle.

But life has its own version of balance. Yin and yang. Light and dark. Just when things rise, something always comes crashing down.

And this time, it took me straight back to the place I had worked so hard to escape.

Another relationship. Another turn I didn't see coming.

It happened fast. A drunken night. A disagreement. Then an explosion of rage.

Before I could even react, teeth sank into my nose.

I felt the bite before I even understood what was happening - the sharp, searing pain as I stumbled backward, my body crashing into the bin. Blood. I could see it. Smell it. The shock blurred everything else.

The next moments were a haze.

The police arrived. A statement was taken. I was handed several numbers - resources, helplines, things that were supposed to help. But I wasn't even there mentally. I was floating somewhere outside of my own body, watching it all unfold.

It was serious. Which meant court.

But this time, it wasn't just me.

This time, my children were involved.

They hadn't seen it happen, but they had been there - close enough, involved enough, for the court to insist they attend.

Absolutely not.

There was no way in hell I was dragging my daughters through that. We were healing. We had come so far, just the three of us, and I refused to let them be pulled into a system that didn't give a damn about the scars it left behind.

I went to court.

And I dropped the case.

Maybe some would say I shouldn't have. That I deserved justice. But I wasn't thinking about me. I was thinking about them.

I had saved them from any extra trauma.

But in doing so, I had enhanced my own.

Because being back there - back in a courtroom, reliving everything I had buried - was like having old wounds ripped open.

My head was a mess.

I walked out of that courtroom knowing I had done the right thing for my daughters.

But I had sacrificed a part of myself to do it.

And now, every time I looked in the mirror, I had a scar to remind me - a physical mark, etched onto my skin, to match the ones I had been carrying inside me all along.

Other people's unhealed shit. They don't just leave bruises. They don't just hurt you in the moment.

They leave lasting damage.

And from the past to the present, I was now completely drained.

But even with the weight of it all pressing down on me, there was one thing I knew for sure.

I wasn't done fighting yet.

Because I never was.

Overcoming all of this wasn't easy.

Facing the shit you try to bury, the memories you've locked away so tightly you convince yourself they don't exist - that's the hardest thing you'll ever do.

I tried to avoid it. I really did.

In my early thirties, I turned to antidepressants, hoping they'd take the edge off. But one day, I arrived at work with no recollection of how I even got there. My brain was numb. Detached. I think I cried and then, just as quickly, I felt nothing.

That's when I knew.

I couldn't mask things anymore. I had to face them.

That's when everything started to shift.

I was introduced to EFT tapping therapy, and for the first time, I opened up about everything. The wounds, the trauma, the parts of my story I had never dared to say out loud. And with that, my spiritual journey began.

It started with a book - The Secret.

Then came the mindset work. The YouTube videos, the audiobooks, the positive affirmations. I plugged into everything that could elevate me.

And it worked.

I acknowledged my past. I wrote letters to the people, the pain, the versions of myself that had suffered. And then, one by one, I watched those letters burn in the fire.

The flames consumed them, and for the first time, I felt something shift. Powerful. Liberated. Unstoppable.

I dove deeper - reiki energy healing, weight training, spiritual practices that rebuilt me mentally, physically, and emotionally.

No one knew what was happening behind the scenes.

On the outside, I was the businesswoman. The single mum. The strong one.

But on the inside, I was rebuilding from the ground up and learning to love myself fiercely.

I didn't stop there.

I studied EFT therapy and reiki, earning my diploma and working up to reiki master level - because healing isn't just about me. It's about helping others.

I started writing.

I had always loved storytelling as a child, but I never expected it to become part of my healing. Then, one night when I was homeless at Christmas, sleeping in a new home we had just secured, something shifted.

I sat in the dark, my daughter sleeping beside me, and a rhyme started playing in my head. A story.

I don't know where it came from, but I knew I had to listen.

I grabbed my phone and, between midnight and one o'clock in the morning, I wrote my first children's book.

I told a few family and friends, and their encouragement pushed me forward. I found an illustrator, self-published, and on launch day, it took off.

Then came the second book, inspired by the impossible - my cat returning home after being missing for two and a half years. The day he walked through the door, I looked at him and asked, "Where have you been?"

And just like that, another rhyme started in my head. Another story was born.

I took those books into schools, reading to children, sharing the magic of storytelling. And in those moments, I felt something incredible - purpose.

I kept writing, whenever inspiration struck.

Then, after my granddad passed away suddenly, I felt the urge to create something different. Real life with a twist of fiction. Laughing through the chaos. A kind of self-help book with added fucked-up life situations from a single mother's perspective, just like laughter therapy to make light of life's challenges.

He would always call me his philosopher, always tell me I was a light in the world - I know he sent me that book idea. I felt it.

And you might be reading this thinking, "Fuck's sake, how does someone get through all of this?"

I'll tell you how.

You just do.

You can. You will.

There's no rewind button in life. No way to take back the things you've said or done, no way to undo the pain that's been inflicted on you.

But that's the whole point.

You grow.

You become.

You break the generational cycles of hurt so the ones that come after you don't have to carry the same weight. It's a little lighter.

As you heal, you start to understand - people don't just hurt others for no reason. They do it because they are carrying their own wounds.

That's why healing is never just about you.

And now? This journey has led me here.

I've hosted an event with Ian Rankin, the legendary Scottish author. I've shared my story of trauma and healing on stage in front of audiences to help others feel seen.

And now, I'm stepping into my purpose - coaching, retreats, and helping others rise any way I'm called to.

This is exactly where I'm meant to be.

And my answer is yes to all of it.

As long as I can spread my good energy.

As long as I can show others that they, too, are unstoppable as fuck. My growth journey will keep evolving, and I'll embrace it all.

Because what they called trauma? I call it fuel.

And I'm just getting started.

## ABOUT THE AUTHOR

# MICTHELLE HOGG

SCAN TO KNOW MORE

***Michelle Hogg** is a solo mum, truth-teller, and bestselling author whose raw honesty transforms pain into power. After surviving childhood trauma, domestic violence, and homelessness, Michelle rebuilt her life through healing, writing, and fierce determination. Her book Finding Life's Meaning In Your Mum Pants! combines profanity with profound wisdom, offering hope through humour. As host of The Whole Hogg podcast, she creates unfiltered conversations about mental health, motherhood, manifestation and the whole hogg! A qualified EFT therapist and Reiki master, Michelle now coaches others through their darkest moments, proving that what they call trauma, she calls fuel. Unapologetically real, relentlessly resilient.*

START OVER VOL 4

CHAPTER

# 10

# Beyond Blood Bonds and Darkness

*The Legacy of Promises*

ROB E WRIGHT

The first three days of my life were spent in a makeshift incubator in my parents' freezing prefab bungalow. The airing cupboard hummed with a gentle, reassuring warmth that fought against the bitter winter chill. My tiny three-pound body lay cushioned among fresh-laundered towels, their cotton fibers still carrying the crisp scent of detergent. The metallic clicking of the heater marked time like a determined heartbeat as my parents kept their exhausted but hopeful vigil, their whispered prayers mixing with the soft sounds of my shallow breathing.

From the start, I was a fighter, determined to survive. At age two, I underwent surgery to remove infected tonsils, followed by four operations to correct a lazy eye muscle. Perhaps these early challenges should have warned me that life would be a struggle, but such wisdom comes only with time. Those trials seem minor now, looking back. In my early primary school years, I excelled academically, showing promise for a future at grammar college.

Sadly, April 9, 1964, was a day that would change everything, and the life of this little eight-year-old would take on a whole new direction. A split second was all it took for a speeding motorist to scoop up this fragile little child and fire me through the air like a little stone from a big catapult. My flight came to an abrupt halt when I slammed uncontrollably into an unsuspecting pedestrian who, until then, was just going about his day. The collision left both of us injured—the unsuspecting man suffered a broken leg, while I had both my fibula and tibia broken.

That day's events would have even more devastating consequences. Though I have no memory of what happened, I later learned I had sustained a cerebral hemorrhage (subdural hematoma) in the impact. The situation was dire—I needed immediate surgery to relieve the blood building up in my skull and pressing on my brain. Though the procedure went well, the surgeon remained doubtful that it would be enough. Speaking to my distraught parents afterward, he apologetically delivered words no parent wants to hear: "I don't think he'll live through the night."

My body temperature soaring, I was packed in ice, and my next fifteen days were spent in a deep coma. Miraculously, on day sixteen I began to respond to stimulation and show the first signs of waking. As consciousness returned, it became apparent that things were not quite as they should be when I discovered, firstly, the new and very heavy plaster cast that now enveloped my immobilized broken left leg, and then the sudden realization that I was unable to move the right side of my body to any noticeable degree. Most frightening of all, my speech had become an almost incomprehensible blur.

The doctors explained they could restore my function through physiotherapy. "When would you like to start?" they asked. "Tomorrow!" came my immediate, though garbled, response. Thus began an endless succession of therapy sessions—pulling sprung levers, lifting weighted pads on my limbs, enduring X-rays and massages. Each set of sessions was followed by assessments that measured my painfully slow progress. All I wanted was to be a normal eight-year-old again: running around, kicking a football, and climbing trees with my friends. That possibility seemed distant, but to me, "possible" meant achievable—and I wasn't going to let that chance slip away. Though I couldn't run toward that goal, I was determined to learn how to walk toward it, no matter how long it took or how small the steps.

Although it may seem something small to most, an inquisitive little seven-year-old girl from the main ward was to have a significant part to play in my journey back to consciousness, my determination to recover and reach my goal, and make this whole traumatic experience nothing more than a distant memory. Seeing me in the side ward at some point during her travels through the corridors had sparked her interest enough to ask about me. Years later, I discovered that this little girl had visited me frequently throughout my coma and continued her visits until she was discharged from the hospital. Learning that I could still hear people speaking despite appearing asleep—with my eyes closed and unable to move or talk—only fueled her curiosity further.

Armed with this insightful snippet, she took it upon herself to come and talk to me whenever possible. Though she knew the conversation would likely be one-sided, my new friend embarked on this personal mission as her way to help, even if just a little. I honestly believe her visits aided my slowly returning speech, as I have many clouded memories of conversations with a voice that I wondered for years was real or imagined. Only recently was this question finally answered—now I not only have a name and face for the voice I heard all those years ago but also someone I consider my little sister and am proud to call a lifelong friend.

Whilst in the coma, I also have a memory, even to this day, of walking through a gossamer tunnel. My back was cold, and it was bright in front of me. There was a smell of wallflowers, and a man was walking toward me. "You coming then?" the man said. I looked back at my mother and then turned to the man and said, "I can't leave my mum crying." "Well, go back then, it ain't your time yet," he told me. I didn't recognize him, but years later I was with the family on my uncle's farm during haymaking. It was the first time meeting my uncle, so my father introduced us. "This is your uncle Ern," to which I replied, "Blimey, he looks just like the man I met in the tunnel when I was unconscious that sent me back." My father then said, "That must have been my dear old dad then, because your uncle Ern looks just like him."

Eventually the day came when they allowed me to go home. It had taken over three months but, after multiple changes to the cast on my left leg, brain function checks, psychiatric monitoring, countless counseling sessions, and enough powerful pain medication to open my own pharmacy, it had felt like three years.

I was so happy to be home, thinking the difficult part was over—but I was wrong. The severity of my injuries had affected both my body and brain, transforming me into a very different little boy from the one who'd left for school that fateful day. My whole demeanor had changed, my leg remained in plaster, I had a wonky eye, very limited mobility on my right side, and my speech was slurred and people struggled to understand me. I became a frustrated and angry child, prone to outbursts and temper tantrums. As the middle of three boys, my being barred from returning to school by medical professionals and education authorities only made things worse. Other than Trina, our family Alsatian, who would patiently listen for hours while I vented my frustrations, there was only my father who seemed able to understand me—not just verbally, but physically and mentally too.

I spent each day of the following six years riding shotgun with my father in his lorry. At the risk of losing his job as a coalman, he would take my education down an untraditional route. Teaching me the conventional reading, writing, and arithmetic, dotted with lessons in history but also the more unusual lessons for life itself. I learned about the laws of the land, weights and measures, and all the while I had an ever-increasing love of the natural world and the beauty of nature, which later developed into a love of writing poetry.

The family moved into a much larger, newer, and warmer house than the tiny little prefab, so we sardines had a bigger can. I'd been given a box brownie camera. The new house meant more room, and my new camera gave me an interest in photography. All the beautiful things seen while out with dad I could now photograph and make into a memory I could see whenever I wanted rather than those moments being lost in the sands of time forever. I had the tools and all the passion in the world, but skill and knowledge levels that were vacuous in comparison, so now all I had to do was learn how to use it.

Sadly, the inevitable happened, and dad was sacked. While working his fill-in job as a milk delivery man, I would also ride with my father, but this was cut short when dad again changed jobs because unfortunately I wasn't permitted to go with him. So there went my chance to get out to see things I wouldn't normally see, and with it went the chance to hone my photography skills and take more than the handful of slightly blurry shots in my tiny collection. Without the opportunity to practice, my photography was put on the back burner. It would only resurface again over fifty years later when just by chance I would finally meet my very own Mr.

Miyagi in a guy called Andy, who would become a mentor for my photography and a great friend.

At 11 years old, the employment service had told myself and my mother that I wouldn't have to work due to my medical history and should claim all the state benefits possible and have an easy, gifted life. Now only a year from that being a possibility made it a very bitter pill to contemplate and one I wasn't about to swallow easily. I was determined to prove them wrong, so I did odd jobs around the neighborhood.

Despite progress since the accident, I still struggled with anger, especially after losing Trina, my trusted canine confidante. To manage my emotions, I found solace in writing poetry. Though my psychiatric assessments continued, and I was prescribed Valium, few knew the true source of my distress—relentless bullying from my eldest brother and local teens who mocked my slurred speech and differences.

The bullying from my older brother then took a more sinister and terrifying turn when the abuse went from verbal and physical to sexual abuse. The increased mental torture of this whole new level of abuse I was being forced to endure would eventually take such a toll on me mentally that I could see no solution other than to take myself out of the equation and end my own life. In my mind, the Valium would become my savior, but not in the way neuro-consultants had intended. I stared nonchalantly at the mountain of yellow tablets and then I was staring at the empty space left behind in my palm.

Fortunately, or unfortunately, depending on your point of view, my mother was to end my dream of escape when she saw the empty bottle and realized that I had just finished swallowing what I thought were the nails in my coffin. "Oh my god, what have you done!" she screamed, and with that she called an ambulance. I was rushed to hospital where I was to have my stomach flushed and spend the next three days recovering under observation.

"Whatever possessed you, boy?" asked dad when I got home. Learning the truth, he exploded with fury. My mother and two brothers bore the full brunt of dad's anger and were told in no uncertain terms, "This stops now!"

That's the end of it, I thought, once and for all. I couldn't have been more wrong. Yes, it calmed down for a while, but it didn't take long before it started again, and it was again reaching the point where I just couldn't take it anymore.

I was fifteen and working at a company with my dad and his youngest brother Len—a perfect situation that I thoroughly enjoyed. Unfortunately, my elder brother worked there too. One day, when he rubbed a mixture of liquid gas and red diesel into my eyes and face, I reached my breaking point. My body filled with unbridled, uncontrollable rage. Suddenly, the four years between us meant nothing. I hit him again and again, each punch harder and angrier than the last, until my father stepped in to stop my frenzied—but I believe justified—retaliation. After learning about my brother's endless beatings, my father's voice boomed out: "The big brother bullying will stop, as you've met your master." Those words still ring in my ears as clearly as if I'd just heard them. I couldn't tell him that bullying wasn't the only torture that had resumed—it would have destroyed him. I kept it buried inside, only revealing it now because it cannot hurt my dear old dad—God rest his soul.

My eldest brother hated me, and my mother tolerated me with a cold acceptance, but he never laid a finger on me again, although at the time I wasn't to know I would be free. I had to find a way out, and my last try was an unmitigated disaster, so leaving home seemed to be the only other option.

I moved away into my own safe space, and I attempted to enlist in the Army but failed because of my medical history. About a year later, I cheekily tried again using an assumed name, and this time I was successful. I spent the next 4 years doing my bit serving queen and country and wore many bruises and black eyes after taking up boxing for the regiment but now bear the scars of a nail bomb incident and a ricochet bullet that I received in the course of my duty to the crown. Sadly, after my name indiscretion, real identity, and consequently medical history was discovered, I was discharged with immediate effect… quietly.

At a loose end and sporadically filling time, I married a girl that I'd met and moved to London, and we had a child a year into the marriage. Not a good idea, you might say, and you would be right!

Turns out she was a former prostitute from the exact area we now resided. It doesn't take a genius to work out the marriage was doomed to failure, and we were soon divorced, so I took my son and made the decision to move back home to live with my parents. A decision that was made easier knowing my elder brother had also married and was now living with his wife in their own property.

After my divorce, social services stepped in and attempted to have my son adopted. I took my case to the county court and succeeded, but the victory was short-lived when social services then applied to the London Court of Appeal and won. I had the case referred to the House of Lords but, incredible as it may seem, was refused on the grounds of the social services recommendation that my brain injuries were severe enough to warrant me an unfit father. That was the last contact I ever had with my son before he became yet another casualty of a cruel system, and I was left with nothing more than my memories and a name on a piece of paper.

To keep my mind occupied and ward off dark thoughts, I pursued new interests, learning judo and karate but gave up boxing and took up football because I decided it was better to kick leather rather than eat it. I earned my HGV 1 license and began a career in long-distance haulage across Europe in 1979. My routes took me from delivering bacon and benches to bringing back tires and machinery. However, changes in the industrial landscape led to redundancy in 1980.

Not wanting to be unemployed, I went through a succession of short-term jobs. In the same year, I also met my second wife, with whom I had a boy and a girl, and we wed two years later in 1982, which coincidentally was the year war broke out in the Falkland Islands, prompting me to successfully enlist in the NATO-committed territorial army, and yes, it was under my real name. The war was short-lived and over too soon for me to take part, and unfortunately, a year after the war ended, at age 28, my joy at being a military man again was halted when I was caught up in an explosion. The result of which was a life-changing severe spinal injury, and I suffered a second brain bleed, which again led to paralysis of my right side. It also meant I was to wear a caliper on my leg for the next two years.

Being older and because of the residual damage of the previous hemorrhage, I wasn't to be as lucky as before. These two extra factors had a considerable effect, and my healing which was not only slower, but I was also never to make a complete recovery, and I now have a permanent restriction in my mobility and an incredible difficulty in situations where it is necessary to interact with others due to the changes I can experience in my temperament and tolerance. It is something I have now learned to accept, but at the time I was prepared to fend off this prospect, and I tried to get things back to normal.

Getting back to normality meant finding work, but this proved far more challenging than expected. My job applications were repeatedly rejected, creating a growing list of disappointments. I then shifted my focus to volunteering, starting with a first aid refresher course at the British Red Cross. This led to becoming a trainer and assessor after earning my B-Tech First Aid Practitioner and City & Guilds Trainer/Assessor N.V.Q. qualifications.

My dedication was rewarded when I was appointed Emergency Response Planning Officer for East Sussex. In 2000, I led an 80-strong team during the Lewes emergency when the River Ouse flooded the lower town, affecting numerous homes and businesses. My role involved managing all British Red Cross personnel, coordinating transport and logistics, and keeping the local council updated on the numbers of homeless, casualties, and available personnel.

Pressing the radio closer to my ear, trying to hear over the chaos: "We're losing ground fast!" The urgent call crackled through my radio as the murky waters of the River Ouse crept higher.

As the flooding spread, we had to relocate the emergency control center to the town hall in the upper part of town. From the control room, I could only watch as the lower town transformed into a Venetian nightmare. I glanced at my team, their faces etched with determination, working tirelessly despite their exhaustion, until eventually the waters had sufficiently receded and finally, I could make my way home after a grueling 19-hour shift.

Unknown to me at the time, I was nominated to meet Prime Minister Tony Blair at 10 Downing Street following the 2000/2001 incident. Standing before that famous black door with its gleaming brass numbers, I felt the weight of history. Inside, the transition was dramatic—from street noise to reverent silence, our steps hushed by thick carpets as we passed the watchful portraits of former Prime Ministers. The atmosphere was heavy with polish, old leather, and the weight of centuries of power and countless decisions that had shaped our nation.

After a brief orientation, we were introduced to Mr. Blair, who sat down with us emergency service representatives for what I can only describe as a think tank session. The meeting was a great success, ending with Mr. Blair congratulating us on a job well done. As we were about to leave through Number 10's grand door, he asked, "Is there anything I can do for you?" I cheekily replied, "Could you lend me ten quid? I can't afford to get home since you've just put the tax up on fuel." He smiled politely and walked away. There went my chance of a knighthood.

After two decades with the Red Cross, my military background opened an exciting door when Major Bob Dodds of the Sussex Army Cadet Force approached me. My heart swelled with pride as he revealed his plan to recruit me as an instructor for young Army Cadets. Though different from my active service days, I jumped at the chance to pass on my knowledge to cadets starting their potential military journeys. For the next seven years, I guided and inspired two detachments of cadets, instilling the discipline essential for military life. I also took on the role of county first aid trainer for the cadet force, teaching both adults and cadets vital lifesaving skills.

Sadly, no amount of medical training could help my second wife Marion when, during my third year with the cadets, she contracted Non-Hodgkin's lymphoma. Five years later, our marriage of 26 years was cut short when in 2008 she passed away. The already strained relationship with my son, who had moved out by this time, then fell apart completely.

This was quickly followed by ties with my daughter, who was secretly bleeding my bank account to the tune of over £3,000 while "supposedly working," all while I stayed at home caring for her young son. Possibly due to my grief at the time and later health issues in 2011 (heart failure and a blood clot in the left lung), her thieving had gone unnoticed. When 6 years later in 2014, I reconnected with a lady called Jen that I'd known from very early childhood and rekindled our teenage relationship, my daughter took my grandson and closed the door, ending contact between us and shutting me out entirely.

My daughter has six children and a grandchild, Oscar, with no. 2 due soon. Though I've met Oscar twice, his father Harvey, like the generations before him, has distanced his new family. I remain a stranger to my other grandchildren and great-grandchildren.

In complete contrast to my ever-diminishing relationship with my family, the love between Jen and I was growing exponentially, and although Jen tried on many occasions to build bridges, each attempt was, to my disgust, either thrown back or maliciously taken advantage of.

Throughout my life, with the exception of a few, I've been treated with contempt. Regarded as a brain-defective buffoon. Rebuffed and ridiculed by many, including friends and family. Jen was different; she saw me differently. She saw the person inside, refusing to let the opinions of others cloud her mind.

One evening, as we sat in our lounge laughing and joking as we would on many an evening, Jen turned to me with that determined look I'd come to know so well. "You know what?" she said, her eyes twinkling, "These poems of yours shouldn't just sit in a drawer. They deserve to be shared." I shook my head. "They're just scribblings, Jen." "No," she insisted, taking my hand, "They're more than that. They're your heart on paper. You should see if you can get them published." The way she believed in me, without hesitation or doubt, made anything seem possible. It was a lovely thought, but to me it seemed like a bit of a pipe dream.

Jen was my reason to carry on. Jen knew my history and the problems I'd lived through. It was her who lifted me up and put life back on track. We were devoted, and the fun we had every day was immense, but in 2016 we were both devastated when Jen was diagnosed with lung cancer. We moved into a new bungalow as it was easier for us both and began transforming it into our perfect little palace.

If there was one thing Jen excelled at, it was organization. Every day brought a constant flow of tradespeople through our new home, each using their particular skills to bring our ideas to life. Who knew that one of these brief connections would also bring into our lives someone who would significantly impact our future? During his time with us, Andy not only helped create our little slice of heaven but also became a fantastic friend to us both. His incredible sense of loyalty and compassion shone through—knowing how precious every moment between Jen and me was, he worked tirelessly to make our lives as comfortable as possible, insisting everything be perfect. Jen was so moved by his dedication that she asked him to promise to be essentially a right-hand man to me when the inevitable time arrived, and she would no longer be able to be there for me in life. A promise he made and has kept faithfully to this day.

And although she fought tooth and nail to fight it for the both of us, Jen was to eventually lose her battle to that terrible disease and sadly passed away in 2021, but not before making me promise her faithfully that should she not survive I was to, in Jen's words, "Carry on as there's no rush, I will be waiting right here for you when it's time." A promise that will be locked in a heart for which only Jen holds the key.

I now watch from a distance as my estranged family gathers, nothing more than a ghost at my own family's celebrations.

The weight of unsaid words, missed birthdays, and absent hugs sit heavy in my chest. Yet through this pain came an unexpected lesson: family isn't always about blood. Sometimes it's about the people who choose to stay, who see past our scars and love us or are there for us anyway. Jen taught me that. Andy reinforced it. Their presence in my life showed me that while we can't change the past, we can build a different kind of future.

Andy, true to his word, not only turned Jen's belief in me and my pipe dream into a reality by helping me publish my first ever book of poetry but also made it possible to include my very own photographs in the book. When he happened to mention that he was a photographer, it reignited a 50-year-old passion, and he began teaching me the art of taking beautiful images, a selection of which now complement the poems in my book.

If only our paths had crossed with Andy a little sooner, Jen may have been with me to experience the overwhelming sense of pride, achievement, and joy I felt when I was able to hold in my hand the very first book in a list of many that I plan to publish as the legacy of my promise to Jen.

Every day of the seven and a half short years we were lucky enough to spend together were, and forever will be, the best days and years of my life, and I shared every single one of them with Jen, who captured my attention as a teenager, stole my heart as an adult, and with whom I would share a love that was and still is boundless and forever.

After a lifetime of adversity and having to prove myself repeatedly without conventional education, I look back satisfied that I've left my mark on the world.

There have been many times when I've had to restart and reinvent myself. I'll never fully understand what it was inside that spurred me on to keep going, but what I do know is that deep down inside all of us, we all have it somewhere. It may be a different thing for all of us, but it is there, and all each of us need is the courage and determination to keep looking for it. Like myself, you may find it without ever knowing you have, but it is there within us all, so never stop looking and never give up the fight, and just as I have, you can overcome anything.

Through my journey, I've learned that true resilience isn't just about surviving hardships—it's about finding purpose in them. My work with the Red Cross, teaching cadets, and finally becoming a published author showed me that each setback can lead to unexpected opportunities for growth.

The loss of my family connections taught me that while we can't control others' choices, we can control how we respond to them. Instead of letting bitterness take root, I chose to channel my energy into creating something meaningful—my poetry and photography.

Perhaps the most profound lesson came through Jen and Andy's unwavering support. They proved that sometimes life's greatest gifts come disguised as simple acts of faith in our abilities. Jen's belief in my writing and Andy's dedication to fulfilling his promise demonstrated that authentic relationships could heal even the deepest wounds.

My transformation from a struggling child in an airing cupboard to a published author shows that our past circumstances don't define our future potential. Every challenge I faced—from early health issues to personal losses—added another layer to my story, making me better equipped to share these experiences with others through my work.

Success isn't always measured by conventional standards. Sometimes it's found in the quiet victories: keeping promises, maintaining integrity through adversity, and creating something meaningful that outlives us. My legacy isn't just in the books I publish or the lives I've touched—it's in proving that it's never too late to reinvent yourself and pursue your dreams.

## ABOUT THE AUTHOR

# ROB E. WRIGHT

*Rob E. Wright is a former military serviceman and dedicated public servant who spent two decades with the British Red Cross. Living in his hometown of Heathfield, East Sussex, Rob channels his passion for life into poetry and photography, having published "The Natural World," a collection celebrating nature's beauty. After overcoming a traumatic accident in his youth, he now inspires others to persevere and achieve their dreams. When not writing or taking photographs, Rob explores the outdoors on his mobility scooter, often accompanied by his friend Andy Corby. Find his work on Amazon or follow his poetic journey on Facebook as "Laird Robin Edward Wright"*

# CHAPTER 11

# She remembered who she was and the game changed

*Silence was their weapon, truth became mine.*

SAM JOHNSTON

I got out of bed, my body heavy, my mind fogged with the weight of something I couldn't name. Walking to the bathroom, I noticed my clothes crumpled on the floor - torn. I bent down, fingers tracing the ripped fabric, confusion pressing against my temples. My head throbbed. The room spun. I left them there and continued walking.

Standing in the shower, the pieces of a puzzle I didn't want to solve began forming. I was swollen. I was bleeding. I shouldn't be bleeding. Bruises mapped my skin - deep, dark imprints where memories should have been. But there were none. Dread rose in my chest, thick and suffocating.

I reached for my phone. Messages. Missed calls. None of it made sense. And then - his name. Tax.

"How's your head?"

"Do you remember much from last night?"

I didn't. I couldn't. The air thickened. My body screamed, but my mind refused to listen.

Another message.

"Delilah is asking if we fucked."

I stared at the screen. Why would my boss's wife be asking him that? No. That wasn't possible. There was no way. I would never. But my body - why did it look and feel so abused?

Panic clawed at my throat. Expecting the worst, I typed the question.

His reply came quick. Laughing.

"Don't worry, we didn't."

"Nothing happened."

"They're just being dramatic. Just asking because you're the new girl."

"Ignore it."

Relief. Forced. Temporary. He said nothing happened. I had to believe it. Because the alternative? Unthinkable. I shoved down the unease, grasping onto the only explanation that fit. They were just being judgmental.

Monday morning brought a moment that would shatter my carefully constructed denial. My boss and the receptionist showed up at my job site. She was never on-site. I knew something was wrong.

They called me over - my boss, the receptionist, my foreman. No greeting. No warmth. Just a single, piercing comment that shattered the ground beneath me

"We don't screw the crew."

Time stopped. My boss's eyes went from blue to grey as he locked onto mine. Dread poured through my veins, paralysing me.

"I didn't." The words left my lips on instinct. But then - doubt. Did I? Why would Tax tell me we didn't if we did? I wasn't even alone with him.

It happened so fast. The words hit me like a slap, and before I could ask why he'd said it, he was gone.

I reached for my phone, my hands trembling. Tears welling up, desperate to remove the judgmental blanket he had just thrown over me.

"I didn't sleep with him. I swear. I would never. We weren't even alone. I respect you. I respect this company. I'm not like that."

The reply: "Sweet as."

My gut twisted. The words felt wrong. His tone was off. He didn't believe me.

I asked my foreman - the only other witness besides the receptionist.

"Why did he say that?"

He laughed as he walked away. "He's just joking. Don't overthink it."

Joking. "That's not a funny joke."

"That's just him. He's winding you up. Let it go."

I wanted the truth. But more than that - I wanted this to disappear. I needed to believe nothing had happened. My body knew something was wrong. My mind was screaming alarm bells. Messages on my phone proved I was angry at him. But I didn't know why. I didn't want to know why.

Shame wrapped its fingers around my throat, silencing me before I could even find the words. I shut down. Trapped in the fog of confusion, I dismissed my intuition, convincing myself it was just a joke. A "joke" I would hear, over and over, for an entire year. From colleagues. From management. A punchline at my expense - mocking a reality I wasn't ready to face.

One year later, the memory of that night struck me like lightning. As if someone had just implanted a memory chip inside my brain, I watched that night play out like a horror film. Scattered pieces, missing frames - but enough to confirm my worst fears were true.

What did you give me? That wasn't what I thought it was. I got dizzy. Really dizzy. I said no. I told you I wanted to go. You grabbed me. My vision blurry. Too weak to walk. Everything went black.

Then - a moment of consciousness. I feel so relaxed. I'm on my back looking at the stars. I can hear the sea, the waves crashing. I look at my hand - it's so light, like it's floating in slow motion. It's so peaceful.

Then - laughter in the background. As I catch a glimpse of a familiar shadow walking away, he's angry, muttering words under his breath. Where was he going? Why was he angry? My head barely able to turn, I try to call out.

A bright light suddenly steals my focus. I see Tax. He's kneeling between my legs, prying them apart, his grip firm, unrelenting. The glow of his phone illuminates me - a spectacle for his amusement. A dick is shoved against my mouth. Laughter continuing to echo.

Panic surges through my body, but my limbs are useless. Deadweight. I try to move, to resist, but nothing obeys me. I tried to scream. No sound. Darkness.

Then - pain. I fought. "Stop! It hurts! It hurts!" I said no. I said no.

His breath in my ear, poisoning me with threats. He tells me he has photos of everything. That if I tell anyone, he will show them. He will hurt me. I will lose my job. No one would believe me.

Then - blank. A blurry face. A moment of safety. But just as fast, they vanished. I was alone, walking the streets. It's dark and raining. My phone ringing. Messages flooding in. People asking where I was. Telling me to come back.

I didn't know where I was going. I just knew I had to get away.

I stayed up all night, shaking. Every message, every comment from the past year now made horrific sense. The floodgates opened to hell. This was real. I felt dirty. I didn't go to work the next day. I went to the doctor. I needed my body checked.

One year earlier: Ripped clothes. Internal swelling. Bleeding and bruised. How did this happen? Why am I only remembering now?

My heart pounded relentlessly, my stomach hollowed by dread. I couldn't ignore it. I felt physically sick. All this time they thought we fucked? All this time I had been saying nothing happened - they knew something did?

I needed the truth. Wearing my heartbreak like an open wound, I messaged my boss's wife and the work receptionist. Separate messages. Same desperate plea.

"Please. I don't want drama. I won't take this further. I just need to know. What happened that night? Why did my boss say, 'We don't screw the crew'? Why did you ask Tax the next day if we fucked? What do you know? What am I missing?"

Nothing. Not even some embarrassing drunk night drama. It was as if the night went off without a hitch. Textbook sympathy, wrapped in gaslighting - they both reassured me nothing happened.

"The mind plays tricks on us." "You know how he is - he just likes to make people uncomfortable." "Don't overthink it." "Don't drag up the past." "You're fine, Sammy."

Sugarcoated dismissal laced with apathy. My gut screamed they were lying. But my heart - my heart wanted relief.

Then, my boss's wife said something that made my entire body still. "Samson doesn't know anything either."

Wait... He doesn't know? The man who made me feel like a whore in front of my colleagues? The man whose judgment I had desperately tried to erase? The man whose approval I had begged for? The familiar shadow in the night, walking away?

If he didn't know... Relief. The weight of an entire year lifted. "They were just joking." "It's fine." "I'm overthinking."

Overwhelmed with gratitude, I apologised. I thanked them. Thanked them for putting my nightmare to rest. Promising I would never speak of this again.

For two years, I kept my promise. For two years, I buried that night. Tax and I no longer worked together, so I barely saw him. The jokes stopped. Everything went back to "normal."

Externally, I was fine. Untouched. Unaffected. Despite the red flags, I convinced myself - nothing happened. But inside - inside I was shutting down memories. Ignoring triggers. Suppressing emotions. Losing my identity. Protecting myself from the truth I wasn't ready to face.

I wore the smile well. Upholding my reputation. "Strong. Independent. Capable of holding my own." But inside - I was in a constant war with darkness. A darkness I couldn't begin to understand. I didn't realise how much of myself I had lost. I didn't see the cracks, the damage buried beneath the surface.

Not until I witnessed my abuser's escalating violence. Not until I saw Tax again. The man who had drugged and raped me. The man everyone swore was harmless. Was now, two years later, my project manager.

I had only ever worked with him in a group. But working one-on-one? That changed everything. The jokes were aimed at me now. His usual loud, sarcastic banter with the guys softened when he spoke to me. Too soft. Too sweet.

Personal questions slipped into conversations. Work compliments turned into "your eyes look pretty," "your arse looked good in those shorts."

I didn't know how to react. It caught me off guard. Awkwardly, I told him to stop, reminding him he had a partner. He just laughed. "Relax, it's a compliment. Lighten up."

Suddenly, I wasn't sure anymore. Had I misread things? Was I overreacting? The doubt crept in, and instead of pushing back, I forced a laugh. Just wanting to smooth it over, to move on. And for a while, he backed off.

But that's how it starts, isn't it? It never really stops - it just pauses. And when it came back, it was worse. Bolder. More calculated.

The comments returned, but each time, they hit differently. His reactions shifted - like he was testing the waters, seeing what would work. Sometimes, he'd apologise, his voice laced with sincerity just convincing enough to make me second-guess myself. Other times, he'd laugh, making me feel ridiculous for even bringing it up. And then there were times he'd say nothing at all, just move on like I hadn't spoken, leaving me standing there, questioning if I was making a problem out of nothing.

But every time, without fail, things would go back to normal. I never saw it coming - how fast it escalated, how unpredictable he became.

Work was swinging between extremes. My mind never stopped. I was constantly analysing, anticipating, trying to stay ahead of his next move. Exhausted. Drained. And yet, I still believed I had control. I saw what he was doing. I recognised the patterns. I was handling it.

At least, that's what I told myself. I had convinced myself that as long as I played it right, as long as I kept my reactions measured, I could keep this from escalating.

Then he made contact.

His hand, slow and deliberate, creeping up the back of my leg. And it was like a switch flipped inside me. I wasn't just frozen - I was gone. My mind ripped away from the present, dragged back to something I had buried, something I had convinced myself was over.

But my body remembered. That familiar panic rushed in, locking my limbs, stealing my voice. I couldn't move. Couldn't speak. I just stood there as dread seeped through every inch of me.

And him? He was watching. Studying me. Waiting to see what I would do. Would I yell? Would I fight? Would I crumble? I could feel it - his satisfaction, his control. And then he smiled. Like he had won. And he walked away.

On site by myself, I sank onto the floor of an empty renovation job, shaking, numb. My body remembering before my mind could catch up. I knew this feeling. I recognised him. The way he made me feel. The way his presence consumed the air, how his touch burned long after he walked away. The way my body reacted before I could even understand why.

Terror. It wasn't just him - it was them. All of them. Every time before. Every moment I had buried, now clawing its way back to the surface.

Like puzzle pieces scattered across the floor - jagged, mismatched. I scrambled blindfolded, trying to make them fit. My memories were resurfacing, but I was still blinded by lies, illusions, and trauma. My intuition screamed the truth. But my world was orchestrated to make me doubt it.

I sat there, tears rolling down my face, completely overwhelmed and confused, my heart barely beating. Frozen in a past I had forced myself to forget. Frozen in a body I couldn't comfort.

I used to think memories worked in a straight line. That the past was something you left behind. But I was wrong. Memories don't disappear. They hide - slipping between the cracks of time, burying themselves so deep you forget they ever existed. Until something - someone - drags them back. And suddenly, you're not just remembering. You're reliving it.

For years, I convinced myself I was overreacting. That maybe I misunderstood. That maybe it wasn't that bad. Because that's what they told me. My employers. My colleagues. The ones who looked me in the eye and swore it wasn't real. That what I felt - what I knew - was just in my head.

I believed them. I trusted them. Until him. Until the moment I saw the past repeat itself - not in memories, not in nightmares, but right in front of me. In the way he moved. The way he spoke. The way he stripped me of my power without ever needing to raise his voice.

I watched it unfold, every sickening detail. The jokes that weren't jokes. The hands that never asked permission. The threats disguised as laughter. "No one would hear." "No one would know."

I had heard those words before - the whisper of a threat against my ear. I had felt this before - trapped, screaming with no sound, knowing that even if my voice did echo, no one would believe me.

I watched it happen - the past and present folding into each other like two sides of the same nightmare. The gaslighting so seamless, I almost questioned myself again. But I wasn't crazy. I wasn't imagining it. This wasn't a misunderstanding. This was control. And I was being trapped - just like before. Only this time, I saw it for what it was.

I began pulling away, trying to create distance, balancing on a razor's edge between defiance and self-preservation. Fear consumed me, but even then, I carried the weight, determined to keep the wreckage from reaching my employer's desk.

Whether I liked it or not, the cracks were showing. I wasn't the silent, compliant worker anymore. I was becoming the problem.

Desperation gnawed at me as I reached out, trying to reconnect with anyone but Tax - trying to bridge the gap he had created. People were noticing, but not for the right reasons.

"Call Tax... not us."

He loved it. He thrived on being in the middle, the orchestrator pulling the strings.

"They don't want you calling them." "You're annoying them." "I'm in charge. You answer to me."

Mentally blocked from management, I went to the extreme, searching for another job, desperately trying to break free from this daily cycle. To regain control. But even that was sabotaged.

After weeks of failed attempts, I stopped fighting. The fire that once burned within me flickered out. I pulled away even further - calling in sick, leaving work during the day. The panic became unbearable. And still, on my reluctant return, he was there - every day, chipping away at the remnants of me, relentless. While everyone else stood by, eyes glued to the wreckage, pretending not to see the flag I was holding.

Backed against the washing machine, I begged him for the last time. "Stop! If you don't stop, I'm going to tell Samson."

My first 'real' threat. For the first time, I saw it - a flinch. And he left.

My boss 'Samson' showed up on-site, shaking his head. "You got grumpy with him. You two need to sort it out."

I never cry. But my eyes filled instantly. He wasn't seeing it. None of them were seeing it. He paused, confused. He hadn't expected this. "What's wrong?"

There was so much. Too much. I didn't know where to start. I was terrified to speak, but I was just as terrified to stay silent. If I kept defending myself, Tax would twist it. Make me the problem. Start spreading lies. I was terrified I would lose my job.

I had proof. My hands shaking... "I'm struggling with him." "But I'm handling it."

Then I showed him. The pictures. The messages. There was no denying it.

His face went blank. He asked if I wanted him to say something... I immediately said NO and begged him to keep quiet. He left. Then rang me 30 minutes later.

For a fleeting moment, I thought he cared. His voice carried anger, frustration - like he wanted to protect me. Like he wanted to put a stop to the behaviour. I wanted to believe it, to hold onto the possibility that someone, anyone, might have my back in this nightmare.

But then came the words that shattered that hope: "I spoke to my lawyer. I can't do anything without your permission."

His tone, the emptiness behind the anger. This wasn't protection. It wasn't courage. It was legal obligation, wrapped in the guise of care.

I just wanted to rewind, erase everything, pretend none of it had happened. But I couldn't ignore how my boss was looking at me now. Distant. Careful. Different.

I hated that feeling. The awkward side glances. The unspoken pressure. Management knew enough, yet, without my consent, they wouldn't act. It was as if the responsibility to fix it all rested on me.

Through their actions, I could see them reading the fine print of policies, ticking boxes, going through the motions. Erring on the side of caution, to the extreme of taking no action. I wasn't a priority. I was just a problem they were hoping would go away. And because of my warped sense of loyalty, I tried everything to make that happen.

The following morning, my phone rang. My boss. "Are you okay to go?"

It was a renovation in the middle of nowhere - the opportunity I had been working towards all year. The last test before I could be signed off. After everything - the torture he had put me through, the emotional rollercoaster, the constant fight to survive each day - I was standing at the threshold of everything I had sacrificed for, everything I had worked so hard to achieve.

But the cost... I was still expected to work under Tax, alone with Tax. I wasn't. God, I wasn't.

I gripped the phone tighter, pulse hammering, throat closing. I wanted Samson to hear it - hear what I wasn't saying. Please. Please don't send me. Please see through this. Please stop this.

I hesitated. A pause long enough to be noticed. Long enough for him to ask again, to push just a little more. But he didn't.

I forced my voice to stay steady. "Yeah, I'm good."

I wasn't. But what choice did I have? This was my shot. My job. My future. Everything I had worked for. If I backed out now, what would that say about me?

I swallowed my silent scream, buried my fear beneath my ambition. And I went.

Every second was harrowing. Tax knew exactly what he was doing. And worse - he wanted me to know. I had spent months trying to rationalise his behaviour. Convincing myself I was handling it. That if I just said the right thing, did the right thing, he would stop. That there was still a line he wouldn't cross.

I was wrong. He never saw a line. There was never a game, never a misunderstanding, never a moment where he was anything less than calculated. He had been leading me to this exact second, stripping me of safety, of certainty, of control - until there was nothing left but this moment.

The unspeakable confession, a serious threat. So calm. So casual.

"Do you know in date rape situations, you can play music to the victim? They'll feel dread and not know why."

Something inside me snapped to attention. "What? Why are you telling me this?"

That smirk. That knowing glint in his eyes. "I've been doing it to you for months."

No. No, this was a joke. It had to be. "That's not funny. Don't joke about that."

"Who said I'm joking?"

"I'm going to fill you up. No one will know, no one will hear you."

Everything inside me started to shut down. He was watching me, waiting, studying my reaction just like he always had.

"Don't worry," he added, tilting his head, his voice almost teasing. "The music isn't playing."

My heart stopped beating. I froze, staring at him, at the man I thought I had been handling. The man I thought I had been fighting off, pushing back, setting boundaries with. I had been so fucking blind.

"What?" My voice barely came out as I stared back into the empty void of him.

For the first time, something flickered in his expression - just for a second. Like he had slipped. Like he had said too much.

"Oh shit," he muttered, shaking his head with a laugh. "I almost gave myself away."

Dismissing that statement like it had no significance. Like my pain, my fear, my entire fucking existence was just a game to him.

"You're so naive, Sam. You have no idea what's going on."

My mind spiralled, every sick, twisted interaction playing back in perfect detail. The way he had tested me, manipulated me, backed me into corners, ignored every 'no' that ever left my mouth. The way he laughed when I pushed him away. The way he studied me every time I froze.

And then - his arrogance slipped. His final, damning confession.

"It's funny," he said, smirking. "The drugs must have worked last time because you don't remember."

"But I did."

And he just confirmed everything. In that moment, every illusion shattered. What he had done... it wasn't my imagination. I wasn't crazy. Taunting me for years, knowing I had no idea.

This was never about me. It was never about miscommunication, or bad jokes, or a man who just wouldn't take a hint. He was a predator. A monster. A rapist. Hunting me from the very beginning.

For the first time, I knew exactly who he was. I was terrified. I've never feared for my life more than I did in those hours. Every fibre of my being screamed to run, but I couldn't - his car was the only way out.

He couldn't know I saw through him, that I was piecing together the fragments of what he'd done. The memories, the moments, the sickening truth all came rushing back, crashing together with brutal clarity.

It took everything I had to hold it together, to suppress the raw panic that threatened to overtake me. The only chance I had to make it through this shift was to remain calm, to play the game until I could get away from him.

That night, the gravity of it all finally hit me. This wasn't just some nightmare I had fabricated in my head. That was a confession - this was real. Everything he had done, everything I had felt, was real.

Four years of torment - too much to process, too much to untangle in one night. So I focused on just that week. That week alone was enough. Enough to expose him. Enough to prove, without question, that he was dangerous. The manipulation, the threats, the way he had made it clear he was a risk to my safety. The fear, the dread, the feeling of being cornered. And most damning of all - the confession. His own words sealing his fate.

In the eyes of employment law, that week held all the evidence needed. A predator admitting to his crime. A pattern of behaviour too clear to ignore.

The words burned as they left my fingertips, but I didn't stop. I couldn't. I had to do this. I had to get him away from me.

The moment I sent the email, a meeting was organised. They wanted to move me - away from Tax, away from the danger. But I couldn't shake the feeling. Instant punishment.

Why was I the one being moved? Why wasn't he the one gone? The thought echoed in my mind, relentlessly: They don't believe me. If they did, if they truly understood, he would be the one gone, not me.

Everything Tax had threatened - everything he said I'd lose if I spoke up - was already happening. They moved me back to new builds, demoting me from the role I had fought for. The job I had sacrificed for, the opportunity I had clung to - gone, just like that. I wasn't allowed to speak. Instead, I was left carrying the weight of their decisions, their silence, their failure to protect me.

I wasn't prepared for the questions that followed. "Why did you leave?"

Confused faces searching for answers I wasn't allowed to give. My colleagues noticed the shift in me - how quiet I'd become. I wasn't myself, and they could see it.

The pressure of their constant need for an explanation finally broke my silence. Without sharing too many details, I told a couple of them what had happened - why I'd been moved. They were furious. Protective. Unapologetically on my side. For the first time, I felt something close to safety.

The following day, a letter - passed through the hands of the receptionist. Informal and cold. A meeting had been arranged. Management wasn't happy I spoke. They weren't worried about me. They were concerned about their reputation.

Loading me with burdens and guilt, they shifted the focus. Leaving that meeting, I stopped fighting for what I needed and started trying to accommodate them instead.

I couldn't function at work anymore. I had done everything to keep this contained. But my days, nights, seconds had become unbearable. I needed help. Real help.

At breaking point, and with nowhere else to turn, I reluctantly reached out to a lawyer. That's when everything changed. She was my saving grace. The first person who didn't hesitate. Didn't flinch. She saw it immediately. I didn't have to explain, convince, or beg to be believed - she just knew.

Her response was fast, clear - unshaken. Like this was exactly what it was: serious. Unacceptable. For the first time, someone met me where I was, laid out my options, and put power back in my hands. And for the first time, I felt validated. Not crazy.

Because of her, I did what no one expected. I believed in myself. Choosing to do the investigation.

It should have been us. A team. Unity. But it wasn't. This process would expose the game - the players, the positions, the silence.

The moment I agreed to the investigation, the connection with my bosses and management team vanished. Everything became email. Detached. Distant. Stripped of any humanity.

I felt like I was on trial. Judged. Picked apart. Now, under scrutiny - forced to defend and justify myself just to claim the justice I deserved.

Sitting in a lawyer's office, speaking into a recorder, my voice shaking as I laid everything bare. The abuse. The pictures he sent. The vibrator he mailed to my home. The threats he spoke. The way he touched me. The secrets he told. The manipulation. The threat of rape.

Details of everything - everything except the night he raped me. I wasn't ready to legally expose that. I still didn't think I needed to.

The information I shared in that interview was then sent to my workplace, to him - my entire interview, in black and white, for them to read. The proof I had to show in order for them to do anything.

My worst fears solidified the moment those details reached their hands. No reaction. No consequences. Tax was still at work. Moving through the same spaces as if nothing had happened.

Sleep became a distant memory. Each moment, at work and at home, felt more dangerous than the last. Tax was given time - time to weave his lies, plant seeds of doubt, and tear my life apart even more. I watched as my colleagues slowly picked sides, their loyalties shifting before my eyes. Behind my back, meetings were being arranged - quiet, secretive, orchestrated. I was left out, completely isolated, forbidden to speak while whispers snaked through the corners of every room.

Their eyes spoke words they weren't brave enough to say aloud. I could feel everything - the subtle shifts, the silent movements. My hypervigilance caught every detail, every attempt to hide the truth.

The cold, sickening realisation settled in: the rot ran deeper than just him. Standing there - helpless in disbelief, my heart bled, like a slow, suffocating death unfolding in real-time. Their whole system was designed to let this happen.

After weeks of isolation, panic attacks, and no sleep, Tax quit. Management failed to share that major detail with me. No warning. No ounce of respect... Just a passing message to everyone in our group chat. A post inviting us to Tax's leaving drinks.

A celebration. Not of justice. Not of accountability. But of him.

The investigation, if it ever truly existed, was in that moment over. I messaged them, upset, confused. He was supposed to respond to what I had said in my interview.

After everything they knew, how could they do this? How could they just let him walk? I was relieved he was leaving, but the way they were handling it felt like a betrayal. A celebration? A send-off? It undermined everything. It mocked the entire process.

I told them it was disrespectful. A joke. I questioned their morals - it was clear now that their values did not align with mine.

Minutes later, I was called into the office. Not for support. Not for reassurance. To be reprimanded.

My boss's tone sharp and defensive: "He quit because of this." "He's worked here for eight years; we owe him the respect to celebrate that." "We have a good relationship with him." "We don't agree with what he's done, but we're not going to burn him at the stake." "That's just not who we are."

I sat there, tears streaming down my face, my heart breaking in real-time. They had read everything. They knew. And still - this was their response.

That night, standing in my bathroom, tears streaming down my face as the weight of it all finally broke me. I covered my mouth, desperate not to wake my kids, as my body crumbled under four years of pent-up emotions.

The woman staring back at me was unrecognisable. The strength, the resilience, the independence. The mask I had worn for years had finally fallen. My eyes, hollow, begging for help.

"Stop crying." "Stop hurting." "Please just stop."

I whispered to myself with a heart of anger, desperate for control. "You're fine." "You're going to be fine."

"But I can't do this anymore." "It's too much." "Please, God, just make it stop."

The last bit of hope I had was being ripped from my chest, left to bleed out each day. I was watching people who were supposed to protect me turn against me like a slow, torturous burn.

Their silence spoke louder than words. Their inaction burned deeper than any wound he had inflicted. Why are they doing this? Why aren't they standing up? Why are they treating me like I did something wrong?

I'm telling the truth. But the truth didn't seem to matter. They went to his send-off despite what I had said. Knowing I wouldn't go.

The following week I asked for a meeting with the boys. I wanted them to see the truth. To know this wasn't just a surface-level complaint - it was so much worse. Management refused.

He was gone, but the poison had already spread. The damage was done. Tax walked away with his reputation intact, a new business, and their support. And I was left to pick up the pieces of my life, knowing my own unemployment was just around the corner.

The apprenticeship I had fought for, for four years, through every ounce of abuse, was nothing more than a consolation prize in the end. Disrespected, tarnished beyond recognition.

The abuse - while horrific - was almost secondary compared to my workplace's response.

I hit an emotional rock bottom that left me spiralling - suicidal thoughts, crippling fear, and shock that left me numb. The aftermath of speaking was far more damaging than I could have ever imagined.

Private meetings continued behind closed doors. Discussions about me, without me. Management shared details with my colleagues, details I was never told - pieces of the story I was kept in the dark about.

When I asked questions, when I pleaded for truth, all I got was dismissive responses: "Move on." "It's done." "He's gone." "We've done all we can." "See a counsellor, I can't help you with this."

They scolded me for questioning their morals. Yet in the end, I was fired - an orchestrated dismissal. No closure. No send-off. Gone.

Expected to walk away quietly, with the truth buried beneath a cover story that only protected Tax and their business's reputation. I was jobless. Soon to be homeless. Drenched in depression. PTSD was so bad I couldn't function. I ended up losing everything in a matter of weeks.

It wasn't just the job. It was my life, my identity, torn apart by betrayal at every level.

Hi, my name is Sam Johnston, and let me reintroduce myself. It turns out I'm a bit of a dark horse alchemist. I am not the woman they tried to break. I am the one who stood in the fire, let it burn through every illusion, and emerged untouched.

What they stole from me, I rebuilt. What they destroyed, I reforged. I sat in the depths of hell, stared into the abyss, and said, "You sure you want to come up against me?" Because let me be clear - I wasn't staying there. And I wasn't leaving empty-handed.

In losing everything, I gained what mattered. Clarity. Strength. The unshakeable knowing that I am carried, protected, and guided by something far greater than the systems that failed me. They underestimated me - thought I was just another casualty of their cruelty. What they didn't realise? I am the alchemist of pain. I transmute suffering into wisdom, betrayal into power, and rock bottom into the foundation of my empire.

They took my stability, my career, my reputation. But what they could never take? My mind. My fire. My ability to rise. I didn't just heal - I evolved. I sharpened. I became everything they feared: a woman who sees through the lies, who moves with purpose, who is untouchable in her convictions. And the best part? I did it with grace. With intelligence. With a level of awareness so deep, it rattles those still clinging to their masks.

They thought my isolation was my downfall. Funny. I thrive in solitude. I revelled in the silence, found sanctuary in nature, and reconnected with my children - not as a shattered version of myself, but as their grounded mother. This wasn't a curse. It was a reset. A divine recalibration. While they were busy orchestrating my downfall, I was being prepared for my rise.

Because real freedom? It's not in what we own. It's in what we let go of. And I let go of everything that wasn't meant for me.

I sat with my fears. Had coffee with my demons. Dissected every wound, every betrayal, every moment I had been forced to swallow my own voice. And on the other side of that reckoning? Clarity. Power. Judgement.

I no longer sought validation - I became my own authority. I no longer feared loss - I welcomed it as a cleansing fire. And when it came time to take action, I did so not from rage, but from something far more terrifying to those who tried to bury me: absolute certainty.

I moved. I exposed the truth. I handed over every piece of evidence, not with vengeance, but with the knowing that justice moves in ways unseen. I surrendered the outcome to forces greater than myself, knowing that lies crumble under their own weight.

I didn't need to chase justice - justice was always coming. My only job? To keep walking forward.

And now? Now, I stand not as a survivor, but as a force. My strength isn't loud - it doesn't need to be. It's the kind of power that moves with precision, that shakes systems at their core. I am not just here to rebuild. I am here to rewire. To dismantle toxic foundations and replace them with integrity, accountability, and leadership that cannot be bought or manipulated.

I am not on a pedestal - I'm building a ladder. One that anyone willing to rise can climb. This isn't about me. It's about us. About shifting the standard. About ensuring that no one else falls through the cracks the way I once did. I'm creating a movement.

For businesses that choose ethics over exploitation. For individuals who refuse to be silenced. For communities that understand true power lies in integrity.

This? This isn't a comeback. It's a rebirth. And I'm just getting started.

## ABOUT THE AUTHOR

# SAM JOHNSTON

SCAN TO KNOW MORE

*Sam Johnston is a survivor, mother, and former tradesperson who transformed personal tragedy into a vision of purpose.*

*After enduring workplace sexual assault and institutional betrayal, she refused the usual routes of silence and carved new paths forward. Now an advocate and systemic change catalyst, she is building a new standard that redefines accountability, prevents harm before it happens, and puts ethics at the centre of leadership. Her work shifts systems and reshapes how people understand them, recalibrating mindsets and structures together. A blueprint for transformation, and a force reshaping how systems (and those within them) treat people.*

CHAPTER

12

# Trafficked, Tortured, Triumphant

ELLEN THERESA

Growing up in a family that took pride in its normalcy—adhering to the rules of God, country, and gender roles—was suffocating for someone like me. I felt like an anomaly from the very beginning. At first, it manifested as a quiet whisper, the persistent sense that something was fundamentally off. But over time, that whisper grew louder, more insistent, until it became a dull, constant ache in my chest that I couldn't ignore.

I was adopted when I was two, and though my adoptive parents were loving in their own way, they were also deeply entrenched in their religious beliefs. Christian fundamentalism wasn't just a faith—it was a way of life, a rigid filter through which everything had to pass. I was raised in a home where the Bible was memorized, dissected, and preached from a place of unquestionable authority. There was no room for questioning, no space for doubt, and as I grew older, no room for difference, either. My identity wasn't my own; it reflected what they desperately wanted me to be. This subtle, suffocating pressure to conform slowly began to warp my sense of self.

Every choice, every thought, every action was scrutinized under the harsh, unforgiving light of their faith. I tried desperately to be what my family wanted: obedient, devout, and compliant. But there was a part of me that simply couldn't conform, no matter how hard I tried. In church, I'd hear hushed whispers about boys who were "lost," girls who were "confused," and the miraculous healings God could provide to bring them back to righteousness. The words weren't directed at me initially, but they lingered like warning signs I pretended didn't apply to my own journey.

My growing realization was devastating: I wasn't like everyone else. I was a lesbian, and in my family's world, that was simply unacceptable. I prayed fervently, begging God to change me, to make me worthy, to help me fit into the mold they'd created for me. When my secret inevitably slipped out, I became a problem to be fixed, a broken thing requiring urgent repair.

Church elders called it "therapy." To me, it became a seven-year trial by fire. They began with prayers that seemed to stretch into eternity, the elders' hands gripping my shoulders as if their physical strength alone could extract the "sin" from my soul. Then came the invasive questions—each one laced with accusation and designed to make me confess desires I hadn't even fully understood myself. Each admission was met with lengthy lectures about damnation and how this burden was destroying my family.

During one particularly harrowing session, they forced me to kneel with a Bible pressed firmly against my head, demanding I recite my sins until I felt God's forgiveness wash over me. Their voices bore into me relentlessly when I failed to change, when I couldn't become the person they demanded. The only thing I ever felt was overwhelming shame. The psychological wounds they carved were so deep that I genuinely believed I was fundamentally broken and unworthy of love or acceptance.

If this spiritual abuse wasn't tragic enough, it was simultaneously drilled into me that men were the natural leaders—head of the household, head of society—and my role as a woman was to be perpetually obedient, submissive, and humble. It became crystal clear that my worth as a person was largely defined by how well I fulfilled these restrictive expectations. I learned to see myself as inherently less than men, as someone who existed solely to serve them. Any display of independence or authentic self-expression was strongly discouraged, and I was systematically conditioned to silence my own needs, desires, and boundaries in favor of keeping the peace, honoring "God," and adhering to the rigid structure of male dominance. This toxic way of thinking became so deeply ingrained in my psyche that I didn't even question its validity.

Living and believing like this systematically shattered my mind, heart, and body, leaving me devastatingly vulnerable to abuse I never could have imagined and would never have allowed myself to endure under normal circumstances. For twelve torturous years, I was repeatedly violated through sexual violence at the hands of numerous men. Tragically, my automatic response was to accept it as something I couldn't control, something I fundamentally deserved. The very idea of standing up for myself felt not only foreign but completely sinful—the last thing I wanted was to go against God's will. I wasn't just taught to submit; I was systematically taught to erase my sense of self, to suppress any feelings or impulses that might disrupt the established patriarchal order.

I felt utterly powerless and believed it was my sacred duty to submit, even when that submission was clearly harmful. My body and my very existence became objects for men to use and control at will. I couldn't see myself as deserving basic respect, let alone protection. Everything was so twisted and distorted in my mind that wrong became right and right became fundamentally wrong. I was completely unable to recognize my own basic right to say no, to speak out, or to demand safety and dignity.

It was a slow, insidious erosion of my humanity. It wasn't the dramatic, obvious moments that ultimately broke me—it was the smaller, quieter ones that accumulated over time. The repeated invalidation of my feelings, the systematic gaslighting using the Bible and faith as weapons, and eventually, the normalized sexual abuse. I wasn't seen as a person by these men; I was merely a tool, a body, a symbol of their righteous dominion over the "weaker sex."

Eventually, I reached a breaking point where I simply couldn't stay any longer. I had to escape or risk losing myself entirely. Desperation drove me to run away from my home, where I wandered aimlessly through unfamiliar streets, lost and desperately searching for any kind of foothold. Eventually, I found myself crammed into a small flat with a group of strangers—a chaotic environment that initially felt like a fragile refuge from my past. What once felt like a genuine spark of hope, a glimmer of possibility for positive change, quickly unraveled into one of the darkest and most crushing chapters of my entire life. The weight of despair grew exponentially heavier with every passing moment, dragging me deeper into an abyssal spiral I never saw coming.

The camera changed everything. What began as what seemed like an innocent encounter with a lens quickly became a sinister gateway to systematic exploitation. At first, the promise made by my newfound "friends" of being captured on film actually felt empowering—a rare chance to be truly seen, loved, and admired for who I was. But the initial allure of the camera quickly darkened into something far more sinister. It became a tool not of artistic expression but of control and systematic objectification. I was gradually drawn into spaces I didn't understand, bamboozled by false promises of escape from the suffocating ideals I had grown up with. Each click of the shutter became a devastating trade-off, and I found myself slipping deeper into pornography and ultimately into the nightmare world of human trafficking. The real me was systematically replaced by a distorted reflection I no longer recognized. This new version of myself was again constructed entirely by the twisted desires and demands of others.

The hours stretched endlessly before me, measured not in seconds or minutes but in the faces of countless strangers. Faces marked by need, greed, and complete indifference to my humanity. My body became literal currency, traded again and again like a commodity. Time became utterly irrelevant as my world existed perpetually behind drawn curtains and locked doors. Twelve hours, sixteen hours, twenty? How long does it actually take to break a human being completely? I stopped counting because the numbers became meaningless. They told me repeatedly that I was property, a thing to be rented and used, not a soul to be saved or valued. "Smile," they commanded, and clicked the camera again and again. There was no genuine happiness in this hellish place, only endless misery and degradation.

Traffickers are predators who systematically prey on the brokenness left behind by pain, fear, or desperation. They possess an uncanny, almost supernatural ability to identify those weak spots, working tirelessly and methodically to exploit them for maximum profit. Trust becomes their carefully woven web, spun with calculated precision to ensnare and entangle vulnerable victims. It's not just physical chains that bind—it's carefully chosen words, constant threats, and calculated psychological manipulation that cage the mind far tighter than steel ever could. "Run," they would say with cold confidence, "and we'll find you wherever you go." Their menacing voices echoed endlessly in my head, filling every corner of my thoughts with paralyzing terror. And so I stayed, believing their lies completely, feeling the crushing weight of invisible chains, and allowing them to transform my deepest fears into impenetrable walls I couldn't see past.

The people I was forced to serve came in all shapes, ages, and disguises, each one dehumanizing me further. Some were businessmen in expensive suits that reeked of cologne and dark secrets, their hands cold and efficient as they used my body. Others reeked of alcohol and desperation, their voices slurred as they stammered the name they had given me—certainly not my real name, anyway. To every single one of them, I wasn't real or human, just an object specifically designed to fulfill whatever they demanded. Each encounter carved another hollow space deep inside me until there was literally nothing left to hollow out. I became a robot engineered solely to satisfy other people's lust and twisted desires.

There were no words of comfort from anyone, only the cold, calculating eyes of those who owned me like property. Their gaze constantly weighed me, appraising their investment, their reliable cash flow. Bruises were nothing but unfortunate damages to the merchandise; exhaustion was merely an irrelevant inconvenience to business operations. "Keep going," they barked without mercy. "Everyone loves you!"

But their version of loving me meant only more faces, more hours, more fragments of myself lost in each transaction.

I was nothing more than a pawn in another brutal system that systematically commodified my body and soul, with all boundaries deliberately blurred beyond recognition. For four excruciating years, I was moved from place to place like cargo, pressured to conform to specific physical appearances, maintain the "perfect" weight, and surrender my will completely to meet the demands of others without any resistance whatsoever. What had once felt like validation was revealed to be pure exploitation. The lines between performance and reality faded until they disappeared entirely. Still photographs, once lifeless and silent, were forced into motion, and the real me was systematically replaced by someone I no longer recognized. Each image captured my physical form, yet the essence of who I truly was had vanished entirely. It wasn't just my reflection in the lens that was lost—it was me, completely and utterly.

My body became a prison in which I desperately tried to cope with my reality. I drowned myself in addictions to substances that temporarily numbed the constant pain and fell into toxic cycles of seeking approval in places that could never truly nourish my soul. I developed severe eating disorders in a desperate attempt to exert control over something—anything—in my life. The pain became so unbearable that I attempted suicide on three separate occasions, each time unsuccessful. When I looked in the mirror, I didn't see myself anymore. I saw a complete stranger, someone who had lost absolutely everything that mattered. The years of living in this deathly submission had systematically eroded my sense of self until all that remained was a hollow shell moving through life without any direction or purpose.

It's nearly impossible to explain what it feels like to exist in that kind of raw vulnerability—a state so devastating it strips you of all pretenses and defenses. It's like standing completely alone in the middle of an endless desert, with the sun bearing down relentlessly on your exposed skin. Your lips are cracked and bleeding, each breath burns your lungs, and every step feels like it might genuinely be your last. You know with certainty that if you keep walking, you might die of thirst, but stopping feels even more certain—a complete surrender to the consuming emptiness.

So you keep moving forward mechanically, not because you have any plan or hope remaining, but because survival is an inexplicable strength woven into every human being, an unyielding force that somehow drives you to take just one more step because standing still feels like giving up entirely on existence itself. That was my daily reality: pushing forward out of sheer biological necessity, even though it felt like I was going absolutely nowhere. It wasn't just physical exhaustion—it was spiritual, mental, and emotional desolation, as if every ounce of strength had been systematically siphoned away. Yet even amid that barren wasteland of despair, life has a strange, miraculous way of saving you in ways you least expect.

My rescue wasn't a grand, cinematic moment with dramatic music and heroic speeches. There were no flashing lights, no shouts of triumph echoing through the darkness, no cavalry charging in to save the day. It came in the simplest, most mundane form imaginable: a door left unlocked. Perhaps it was a mistake, or maybe a moment of carelessness on my captor's part. But to me, it represented everything—a tiny crack in the seemingly impenetrable prison of my despair, a sliver of precious light in the suffocating darkness.

At first, I didn't dare believe it could be real. My trembling fingers brushed the knob tentatively, and when it actually turned, my breath caught in my chest. Could it really be this simple? Every instinct told me it was an elaborate trap, but a tiny spark of hope urged me to flee immediately. My heart was pounding so violently I was sure someone would hear it as I pushed the door open, and I froze completely at first, expecting to hear someone rushing after me with shouts and threats. But no one came. The hallway was empty.

I ran like my life depended on it—because it absolutely did. Though my legs burned with effort and my lungs screamed for air, I didn't care about the pain. Freedom had become a powerful sensation coursing through my veins for the first time in years. Every step represented my complete rejection of the chains that had bound me for so long. I didn't stop running. I couldn't stop. I wasn't just running away from something—I was running toward something meaningful. Toward safety. Toward freedom. Toward reclaiming myself and my life. For the first time in what felt like forever, I had genuine hope flickering in my chest.

My escape wasn't handed to me on a silver platter by someone else. I had to seize it with my own hands and make it happen. And I absolutely did. However, the transition from escape to finding real help and support while in a state of complete turmoil is not a gentle hand reaching down to lift you gracefully. It's a brutal battle—a raw, unrelenting fight to claw your way out of a dark, suffocating pit using nothing but your own determination. The journey that followed my escape was anything but easy or straightforward.

Finding support from people I could actually trust took an agonizing amount of time—uncertain, terrifying time when I didn't know who was safe. Healing, I discovered, is not a straight path with clear directions but a wild, unpredictable labyrinth that forces you to stumble through memories and wounds you'd rather forget forever. It's messy, achingly messy in ways that can't be cleaned up quickly. It involves the gnawing fear of being harshly judged for your scars and the desperate longing for someone who can genuinely say, "I see you. I hear you. You are not alone in this."

Living in a cage built entirely from shame and fear was excruciating to confront in therapy sessions. I wasn't ready to face the true depth of my pain—I just wanted to function normally and get on with life like nothing had happened. I wanted my hands to stop shaking uncontrollably and to silence the constant voice of terror that lived in my head. I knew I had deeply dysfunctional patterns and basic life skills that needed to be completely relearned, so I threw myself wholeheartedly into behavior modification techniques.

If I could behave like someone who was genuinely okay, then maybe I could actually become okay, I reasoned. I learned to wake up on time, hold a steady job, get my GED, enroll in university, and wear the carefully constructed mask of composure. I sought support that emphasized practical ways to manage daily life, such as journaling to process emotions, daily affirmations, attending support groups for guidance, practicing meditation to manage overwhelming stress, and having open, honest conversations with mentors to gain clarity. All these approaches were valuable in themselves, and though they helped me survive day to day, they didn't make me feel truly alive. Beneath the structured routines and coping mechanisms, the deepest wounds continued to fester. I needed to go much deeper to reach the taproot of my pain.

The real breakthrough began with a fracture—a subtle crack in the carefully constructed facade that had held my world together for so long. The crack came quietly, in the form of a single, unavoidable question I could no longer ignore: Who am I, really? For years, I had carried destructive messages that fundamentally shaped my identity: Desire is dangerous and sinful. Your body is not your own property. Your voice is defiant and unwelcome. Your purpose is to please God through submission. Women are the weaker sex by design. Men hold all the real power. These toxic words echoed endlessly in my mind, sinking deeper with each repetition until they became my core beliefs.

Breaking free from these psychological chains took enormous amounts of time and courage I wasn't sure I possessed. I had to learn to systematically confront these beliefs and replace them with truths that better reflected the person I was becoming. A major turning point came when I allowed myself to probe deeper by asking a truly cataclysmic question: Was it possible that everything I had been taught was fundamentally wrong? This was a earth-shaking moment that clawed at the very foundation of my existence. It opened a whole can of other dangerous questions. Did God really create me to be a slave and target for men? Was being a woman truly equivalent to being the weaker sex?

What if being a lesbian was actually beautiful instead of fundamentally ugly and sinful?

I could feel myself unraveling internally as layers of long-buried thoughts started to rise to the surface, piercing through the walls I had so carefully fortified over the years. And then, when I least expected it to happen, the dam finally broke completely. The flood came with undeniable force, as years of suppressed truths and stifled emotions had been waiting for exactly this moment to rise. It wasn't chaos, though it certainly felt like it; it was clarity—raw and unyielding—where avoidance could no longer protect me from reality.

This was the first time I allowed myself to truly cry for what I had endured, and I simply wasn't prepared for the emotional deluge that followed. The tears weren't just sadness; they were rage and exhaustion, tangled together in a huge knot I couldn't straighten. My chest heaved with every sob as my body systematically expelled decades of accumulated toxicity. It was terrifying to let myself feel anything so intensely. I had been taught that emotions were dangerous and not to be trusted, and that it was selfish—even sinful—to give them permission to exist.

But I was angry, deeply and righteously angry. I could feel it burning deep within, growing stronger with every breath. I was furious at the church that condemned my love, labeling it a sin worthy of eternal damnation. Angry at the people who twisted scripture, using it like a weapon to tear at my soul. Angry at myself for believing their lies for so long. Angry at the men who reduced my body to an object for their own selfish pleasure. Angry at how I was left unprotected and shunned for years. And most of all, I was angry at myself—for being a woman, for hating that reality and loving it all at once. I despised the weakness the world imposed on me but cherished the strength I was discovering within me. The conflict burned, searing my thoughts into a whirlwind.

Anger eventually gave way to profound grief—an aching void that lived in my ribcage, constantly whispering of all the precious years I had lost trying to mold myself into other people's expectations. For the first time, I let myself sit in the pain without trying to fix it immediately. I let myself remember my childhood without running away from the memories. Sorting authentic faith from systematic control was like picking apart a barbed wire fence; every piece I removed left me bleeding, but it was the only way to truly heal. It was time—finally my time—to validate little Ellen who had been forced into closets not of her own making.

Recreating horrific memories into new, healthier ones is like walking through a completely burned-down forest, gently coaxing new life where only desolation remains. I remember the first time sitting on a couch with my therapist, heart pounding violently, muscles tense, waiting for a blow and violation that never came, until one day I realized I could sit there, breathe normally, and not brace for impact. It was strange at first, like wearing shoes that don't quite fit, but eventually, I started to trust the safety of that space.

Learning to accept hugs and gentle touch was the hardest part of healing. The first time someone tried to embrace me, I flinched so hard they stopped mid-motion, unsure what to do next. Physical contact felt intrusive and dangerous, like a boundary being crossed even though the person in front of me was completely trustworthy. They were patient as I struggled to look them in the eye and unclench my jaw. I was determined not to feel like I was losing a part of myself in this normal human interaction. So we tried over and over, taking small steps. It was like learning to speak a foreign language with my body. This was a slow, painstaking process that took many months, but eventually I allowed myself to feel the genuine affection of another person instead of fearing it.

Over time, I began to no longer feel utterly powerless. I found my voice and stepped into my authentic being with growing confidence, no longer automatically shrinking or apologizing for existing. Being a woman became a celebration of strength rather than a source of shame. For the first time, I was able to make my own decisions and choices. This sense of freedom reaffirmed my inherent value by reminding me that my voice and dreams are completely valid and worthy of being heard and fulfilled.

My body began to move with power—not in physical appearance, but in how it carried me through the world, fluid and truly alive. Learning to feel safe in my own body through reconnecting with it meant reclaiming my fundamental right to have boundaries and to exist fully. I had to systematically unlearn the survival strategies that only knew how to numb or disconnect. I remember like it was yesterday the first time I said no without apologizing afterward. I felt my voice reverberate through my chest, strong and steady. I took deep breaths, feeling my lungs expand fully, savoring the sensation of my cells being activated with strength and health.

Religious deconstruction was a brutal yet absolutely necessary part of my healing—like peeling away the infected skin of a wound. Each layer I courageously shed revealed the tangled web of control that had been disguised as faith. Memories surfaced around church teachings, and for the first time, the words felt like shards of glass cutting through my heart. I remembered hymns that now sounded like chains, their familiar melodies laced with an undercurrent of obligation and fear. I began to question absolutely everything, and as shame whispered that I'd be betraying everything I had known, I had to take the terrifying risk.

I began to rebuild my life from the ground up. This leg of my journey dared me to reconnect with the parts of myself I had buried so deeply. My sexuality and its inherent beauty were finally to be embraced rather than condemned. I sought out spaces where I could breathe freely, untethered from the crushing demands of religious tradition. I was welcomed as me—untamed and whole—where I didn't have to hide the parts of me that had previously felt forbidden. I was allowed to embrace being lesbian without fear of punishment or eternal damnation. I began to explore all of it, letting myself feel the warmth of desire, the giddy excitement of authentic connection. I allowed myself to love and be loved in ways that used to be impossible.

The crushing heaviness that had sat in my chest for years finally lifted, replaced by a lightness I hadn't known was possible. A sense of peace settled within me, replacing years of toxic shame. I began to see God not as a harsh judge but as a loving presence woven into every corner of my existence. The Divine could not be contained by human dogma, and genuine laughter erupted from my soul. My connection to something greater grew along with a sense of purpose that was authentically my own. I was able to live as I was truly created, and the shackles of guilt loosened their grip. The horizon unfolded before me, vast and unrestrained, filled with endless possibilities and the exhilarating thrill of new beginnings. I was no longer a collection of broken pieces but a restored soul who had transformed from merely surviving to truly thriving.

Stepping into genuine freedom felt like standing at the edge of an open field after years of being enclosed by towering walls. The air was sharper, the colors brighter, and for the first time, I could see my rightful place within it all. Yet as liberating as it was to finally walk unburdened, I also realized that freedom carries a profound responsibility.

To simply exist in my newfound light wasn't enough for me. How could I truly honor what I had overcome if I kept it to myself and didn't use it to help others find their way to the light? The shackles I had worn might have been invisible to others, but they were no less real or damaging. Now unshackled, I wanted to use my hard-won strength for those still trapped, waiting for someone to see them, believe in them, and help them rise.

My first entry point was teaching youth in crisis and juvenile offenders. I saw pieces of my own story in their experiences: the shame, the anger, the complete disillusionment with authority. I worked with gang members who had been written off entirely by society, their lives marked by violence and neglect. They were tough on the outside, but inside, they carried the same longing for acceptance and love that I once had.

Through dedicated mentorship, group activities, and shared moments of vulnerability, I witnessed these young souls begin to change fundamentally. Their hardened shells cracked to reveal genuine glimmers of hope. Watching them make better choices and discover their inherent worth became one of the most fulfilling experiences of my life.

From there, my vision grew exponentially, and I began to ask myself: Where else is hope desperately needed? The answer to this question took me on a sixteen-year journey around the globe in over thirty nations, working with a variety of social justice causes. I became both a warrior and a weaver, battling systems of oppression and stitching together shattered lives with threads of grace. In my humanitarian efforts, I worked to rescue and restore victims of sex trafficking in Asia's notorious red-light districts. Partnering with local police and specialized teams, we brought trafficked women and children to safety and connected them with the resources they needed to rebuild their lives. It was grueling, heart-wrenching work, but each life saved was a victory—a powerful reminder that liberation is always worth the fight.

When I first encountered the Garibout Boys in Africa, the depth of their pain struck me like a physical blow. These boys, often orphaned or abandoned at eight years of age, were sold to religious leaders under the false promise of safety, education, and a better life. Instead, they were subjected to horrific exploitation. I worked hand in hand with local organizations to feed these boys, give them shelter, and most importantly, provide them with dignity and love. Though some were forced to return due to systemic challenges, my efforts were not in vain, as a door of escape was revealed, offering them a path to freedom.

Children with machine guns—my heart stopped as I laid eyes on their faces, hardened by war, with eyes hollow, carrying the weight of experiences no child should ever know. Their small bodies, cloaked in military fatigues, seemed tragically out of place. They were trained to kill, and as I looked into their souls, I felt the crushing heaviness of their seared conscience that came from unbearable pain. And yet amid the overwhelming sorrow, there was something else—a flicker of something pure, something human, buried beneath the layers of trauma. It was hope, fragile and tentative, but it was undeniably there. It burned like a candle in the darkness, a reminder that healing was possible. Something was ignited in me, a fierce determination to help them reclaim their innocence, piece by piece.

Beyond rescue efforts, I focused on the foundations of life itself. In villages, I built wells and homes, ensuring clean water and shelter for families. I worked alongside farmers, helping them cultivate crops and provide for their communities. On medical boats, I joined teams to deliver basic dentistry and eye care to remote island regions, meeting people's essential needs while creating connections that bridged cultural divides.

We've all heard of Mother Teresa and the profound impact she had on the world, but it wasn't until I found myself in Calcutta, India, working in her homes for the dying and destitute, that I truly understood the depth of her mission. For months, I witnessed the raw brutality of women who suffered from leprosy. It struck me like a wave—women with skin peeling from their faces, their bodies deformed and broken, some sitting in dimly lit rooms, others lying motionless on beds, their limbs ravaged and gone. The air in the room was thick with the scent of decay, yet it was the profound stillness that pierced my soul. My role was to sit with these women and demonstrate love by cleaning their wounds.

One day, a sister of mercy asked me to hold orphaned children who were clinging to their last threads of life, succumbing to malaria. Two small boys, no larger than the span between my wrist and elbow, were brought to me. Their bodies were emaciated; their bellies bloated—a cruel mockery of what should have been the fullness of life. As I cradled them in my arms, I felt their fragile frames shiver, their skin cold and slick with sweat. I rocked them, back and forth, back and forth, as the minutes felt like an eternity. The weight of their lives felt impossibly heavy and heartbreakingly light. I wanted desperately for them to live, to feel the breath of life, but I knew in my heart that it was slipping away. I tried to fight the tears, but as compassion welled forth, I knew my tears were a symbol of an exchange, an unspoken bond—their exhale for my inhale, a connection between life and death that transcended words.

Advocacy called me to stand beside the LGBTQ+ community, where their identities cast them into the shadows, leaving them vulnerable to harsh realities. The work was immense, navigating loads of hostility and fear, but the reward was worth every challenge. I created sanctuaries of safety where warmth replaced judgment and the air felt lighter. Everyone was accepted completely, and supporting them as they embraced their true selves was a profound honor and privilege.

I was stationed in the Philippines when the COVID-19 pandemic hit, and as the country began imposing military lockdowns, everything around me shifted dramatically. I had to leave, no longer able to continue the work I had been so passionate about. It was a difficult and sudden departure from a life I had dedicated myself to, and I was left wondering: Now what? I was at a complete loss and took the next eight months to reconfigure my life. Little by little, I felt the universe nudge me in a different direction.

Advocate of Soul was born, leading me to become a certified life coach and mindfulness expert specializing in healing religious trauma. I now guide individuals through the complex challenges of religious deconstruction, helping them uncover and transform subconscious beliefs shaped by harmful doctrines. Through my six-month course, I offer practical tools for growth and empowerment.

My work has come full circle in the most beautiful way. I've authored the AS IS Trilogy (unedited journal writings) and host REAL TALK events that inspire people to reclaim their lives authentically. On the Advocate of Soul Podcast, I provide a safe space for individuals to share their stories and find genuine community.

If you're reading this, please know that your story matters deeply. Pause and take a breath; feel into the simple fact that you are alive, because it matters greatly. Every decision is an opportunity to create the future you envision. Recognize that your struggles are part of your story but do not define your worth or your future—you define you. Understand that when you feel broken, there is a strength within you, waiting to emerge. Moving forward doesn't require perfection; it begins with one brave step. Trust that the ground beneath you will hold you as you move forward. Acknowledge that your fears are not unbreakable; they are shadows that fade when confronted with courage. It's okay to feel like change is impossible because many have felt the same, but take the risk to believe for better days. Remember, you are not alone; there are people who want to help, guide, and lift you. You can move beyond the darkness of this moment, where a future filled with peace awaits you. View your scars as signs of survival and resilience, not failure; they carry wisdom and healing that inspire and guide others. Embrace your worth, knowing that your light is needed in this world.

With all my heart, Ellen Theresa

## ABOUT THE AUTHOR

# ELLEN THERESA

SCAN TO KNOW MORE

*Ellen Theresa is a survivor-turned-healer who transformed devastating trauma into global impact. After surviving religious fundamentalism, conversion therapy, and human trafficking, she reclaimed her sovereignty and dedicated her life to liberation work. As CEO of Advocate of Soul, Ellen specializes in healing religious trauma and empowering individuals to break free from oppression. Through transformative coaching, speaking, and her AS IS Trilogy, she guides clients to embrace their authentic selves unapologetically. Her sixteen-year humanitarian journey across thirty nations—from rescuing trafficking victims to supporting LGBTQ+ communities—demonstrates her unwavering commitment to justice. Ellen's story proves that our deepest wounds can become our greatest gifts.*

CHAPTER

# 13

# A Reclaimed Soul

*How I Took Back What Was Stolen*

ANDREA BEVAN

You may be triggered by my story, as what happened to me shouldn't have happened to anyone, but you will learn how I had the courage to face my past, break free, and not just survive but turn my life around and thrive.

From the age of eighteen months, I lived with my mum and grandparents in a tiny two-bedroom council flat on the outskirts of Salford, Manchester. My mum's marriage to my dad had broken down, and she had moved back in with her parents. This was the last I saw of my dad growing up.

I enjoyed living with my grandparents and have fond memories of going for long walks with my grandad. We would pick blackberries that grew wild on the roads nearby, and my nan would use them to bake pies. Even though we had nothing, this home was a place of love and joy throughout my childhood, and I am so grateful for these memories.

For as long as I can remember, I have loved music, dancing, and singing, and I would put on shows for the family, bringing smiles to their faces.

After a couple of years, my mum got married again. I was around five years old. They bought a house in the same area as my grandparents. Around this time, I started to call my stepdad Dad, and honestly, I don't remember a time I didn't call him Dad. I was too young to remember my biological dad, and my mum and he were no longer in touch.

A couple of years later, my mum was expecting another child. I was around six or seven, and I was so excited and looking forward to having a brother or sister.

When I was little, I spent a lot of my time between my mum's, aunt's, and grandparents' houses; I was close to them all and enjoyed the times I spent there. However, one day, while I was at my aunt and uncle's house, my mum, her cousin, and my aunt were all sitting outside in the back garden. My uncle was in his shed, and I was playing outside. I must have been five or six years old at the time.

While I was playing, he shouted for me to hide in the shed, like the game of hide and seek, so I went inside to hide. I still remember the smell of that place: wood shavings, dirt, oil, tobacco. He smoked heavily, cigarettes, and a pipe. I remember the noise outside of everyone talking, laughing, and having a good time. I stood in the doorway, asking where I should hide, and he said, "Here next to me. We're going to play a different game now," he said, "but you need to be very quiet." This was my first memory of the abuse.

The abuse became the usual whenever I went around,our game and our secret, never to be spoken of. Slowly, I began to change. I no longer wanted to perform shows for people or sing and dance; I no longer wanted to be seen or heard.

Sadness became my constant companion, and I felt lost, as though the person I once was had been stolen, leaving behind only an empty shell. My dreams, my happiness, my very sense of self slipped further and further away. All that remained was the desperate struggle to survive this endless, unbearable nightmare.

My mum worked hard and had a good job, but money was always tight. My stepdad spent a fortune at the pub, drinking ten to fifteen pints a night, often followed by whiskey.

Looking back, it was clear that this was the beginning of his struggles with alcoholism.

The drinking and addiction turned him into an angry, selfish, and volatile man. His need to feed his habit consumed him, and when money ran low, the arguments would erupt. Shouting filled the house, and I would watch helplessly as my mum's face crumpled with sadness and frustration. She must have felt so powerless, trapped in a situation she couldn't control. I could feel her pain.

At just ten years old, the weight began to take its toll. The drinking, the relentless fights, the sexual abuse, it all started to wear me down. Anxiety took hold, making my heart race and my mind spiral. It wasn't just emotional anymore; it was physical, suffocating, and inescapable.

But in the midst of it all, I had one refuge,my grandparents' flat. It was my sanctuary. Within those walls, I felt safe and loved. I spent as much time there as I could, clinging to the happiness and security it gave me.

I was eleven years old when my grandad fell ill. He was rushed to the hospital with a suspected heart attack. He was admitted and stayed there for several weeks.

One night, June 18th, my mum called me in from playing. She was crying and began to tell me my grandad had died; he had suffered another heart attack and had not recovered. I was utterly heartbroken and inconsolable. My mind was spinning. What now? Who would save me from this nightmare?

After the funeral, we went back to my auntie and uncle's house, where there were a lot of people. I remember sitting in a corner by myself when my uncle put his arm around me and said, "Look, don't worry, I can be your grandad." At that moment, anger surged through me as I shouted in my head, "My grandad would never do this; he was kind, gentle, and patient. You are nothing like him. You are horrible, and I hate you." That was when it hit me that what was happening to me was wrong. It shouldn't be happening, and I hated it.

A part of my soul was buried that day with my grandad, along with love and hope. I know if anyone could have helped me and made things better, it would have been him. Now, he was gone, and I was alone in my nightmare.

The abuse continued, along with the secrets and lies, and I didn't want to burden the family with any more pain and upset, so I chose to bear the weight alone, sacrificing myself bit by bit.

I had started to get sores underneath. I can't remember exactly when this started, but I am pretty sure it was around the age of eleven. The incessant itching drove me to the point of bleeding. I would have salt baths, hoping to alleviate the pain, but the relief was temporary. Eventually, when I couldn't take the agony any longer, I mustered up the courage to show my mum. She bought some cream from the chemist to see if it helped; despite the physical pain and discomfort, the worst thing was the overwhelming shame.

I felt dirty and tainted, not understanding what was happening to my young body. It was undeniably one of the darkest chapters of my life, a time marked not only by physical discomfort but also by the shame of someone finding out the horrible truth.

The sores persisted, and eventually, my mum took me to see the doctor. I had mixed feelings about visiting the doctor. On the one hand, I was terrified that he would be able to tell what was happening to me, yet on the other, I had hope that he would somehow rescue me from my nightmare. However, the doctor simply examined me and prescribed creams and lotions. I was confused; why could he not see the severity of what was happening to me? Why was he not helping me? Was this normal? Was I overreacting?

Dad's trips to the pub became more frequent, and it was clear now that he was an alcoholic. It was heartbreaking to watch. He was talented and good at his work, but he couldn't stay away from the drink.

Every day, I dreaded coming home from school, never knowing what lay behind the door, and the uncertainty was unbearable. Often, I'd find him passed out in the chair, sometimes with a lit cigarette in hand or having soiled himself. He'd demand I wake him before Mum got home to avoid arguments, and his mess became my responsibility. If I were late home, he would explode, blaming me when the fights started.

I felt like everything was my fault, like it was my job to keep the peace, to keep everyone happy. But nothing I did was ever enough.

The memory of this one particular day haunts me still, a bit more of my soul stripped away. Mum asked me to go to my auntie's house for some reason; I can't recall why. I said no, adamant that I didn't want to go, but she insisted, leaving me no choice.

Somehow, my intuition told me my aunt wouldn't be home, leaving me alone with my uncle. The fear, panic, and helplessness were overwhelming as I wandered around the streets, desperate to avoid the inevitable.

I couldn't find an escape route, no way to avoid my fate. I was going to have to go and hope and pray she was there, and if not, then so be it. I resigned myself to the harsh reality that this was my life and that I had to endure whatever came my way.

My worst fears were correct when my uncle opened the door, only revealing my aunt's absence once I was inside, trapped, with no way out, no escape, and nowhere to run. It was a stark realization that I was powerless, voiceless, and defenseless. That day, I lost a part of myself, replaced by a broken, hollow shell.

At school, I struggled. Homework was left undone, I avoided classes, I was slipping away, a lost soul. To escape, I drank, first on the streets, then at school. Alcohol was easy to find; my dad brewed his own, and our house was always stocked. Drinking numbed the pain, the confusion, and the feeling of being lost.

I chased excitement, mistaking it for happiness. I slept in squats, surrounded by drugs, and desperate for acceptance, for a sense of belonging. But with every bad choice, I drifted further from myself, sinking deeper into self-loathing.

At fifteen, I met an older boy. He made me laugh, and I really enjoyed spending time with him. We spent most of our time at his house, alone. When he asked me to have sex with him, I said yes. For the first time, I felt in control of my body.

But the feeling didn't last. Over time, he became possessive and controlling. We constantly argued, broke up, and got back together. Meanwhile, he had other girls, and they made sure I knew. But I didn't care. It wasn't the worst thing in my life. I felt wanted and loved, and that was enough, and I loved him unconditionally.

One night, we went to his friend's flat, had drinks, and played music. My boyfriend left for the shop, and his friend stayed. When he returned, he pulled his friend aside, whispered something, and then left again. His friend came back into the room and motioned towards the bedroom. I refused. He insisted, saying my boyfriend had given permission. A voice inside me whispered, "He wouldn't do that," then another said, "Fuck yes, he has." I didn't fight. What was the point? I didn't have a "no" in me.

During this time, I had become distant from my family, and my intuition was telling me that something wasn't right, that I didn't belong, that I had never belonged. I started to think that I could be adopted. I don't know; maybe I was mistaking my feelings with looking for a way out or some normality. I am unsure, but it was there, telling me something wasn't right.

One night, summoning all my courage, I went downstairs. My stepdad was at the pub, and I blurted out, "Mum, why did my name used to be Bevan, and no one else was?" She told me to sit down and said, "Your dad is not your biological dad." Shock washed over me as she continued to reveal to me that she had been married before. Their marriage ended when I was eighteen months old, and he had moved away and worked in various countries.

I was dumbstruck. Somewhere deep down, there was a faint hope that there might be someone out there who could save me from all of this heartache, someone who truly loved me. Yet at the same time, I was fighting an identity crisis. Fuck, who am I, and how does all of this affect me now? Who is who, what is what, and how was this kept a secret from me all these years by everyone in my family, all the people I was close to, lying to me?

I felt fear and panic all over again, completely out of control. What other lies and secrets are out there that no one is telling me?

Was this all I was? Had I let myself become this, or was this what others wanted me to be? Would this define me forever? I realized I had to make a choice: stay and make the best of my current life, or break free and create a new one on my own terms. So I walked away from home, from the life and relationships that were holding me back.

This was the first turning point in my life. I found a job, surrounded myself with new people from all walks of life, and began to see the possibilities ahead. A career, financial independence, the chance to explore the world, things I once thought were out of reach. For the first time, I wasn't just surviving; I was building a life of my own. And with that came something I hadn't felt in a long time: hope.

One weekend, the girls from work invited me on a night out in Manchester. At first, I hesitated, as stepping into the unknown felt daunting, but I faced the fear and went. We started at a local pub, then moved on to a nightclub. The music, the energy, the laughter and the friendship, it was amazing. For the first time in years, I wasn't just existing; I was living.

These nights became more than just fun; they became a new life. With each month, my confidence grew. I took pride in my appearance, held my head higher, and stepped fully into the light. I was no longer just a survivor; I was reclaiming my joy. Surrounded by friendship, laughter, and music, I felt something I had long thought impossible,I felt freedom. I felt like me again. And I was happy.

At eighteen, I found out I was pregnant. It was a moment filled with both excitement and fear. The journey wasn't easy. At twenty-seven weeks, I started bleeding and was rushed to the hospital. Though the bleeding eventually stopped, the fear lingered. When it happened again at thirty-two weeks, I was terrified. Guilt crept in, thinking that I had done something wrong, that I hadn't protected my baby enough.

I couldn't shake the thought that the past abuse had something to do with it. I wanted to tell the doctors, to explain everything, but the words wouldn't come. Then, in the fear and uncertainty, he arrived, my beautiful baby boy, all 8lb 11oz of him. I named him Nathan Allen. Nathan, a gift from God. Allen,after my grandad, the man who had been my rock.

The moment I held him, nothing else mattered. The fear, the doubt, the pain of the past, they all faded in the presence of this tiny, perfect life. I knew, with every part of me, that I would raise him to be strong, kind, and full of the love I had always longed for. He was my reason, my light, my greatest gift. He was my savior, and I was starting to see my soul again.

At twenty-two, during a routine smear, the test showed borderline cancer cells. I had to go to the hospital for tests, and all was not well. They said they would have to do some sort of procedure and have a deeper biopsy taken to rule out further cancerous areas. They insisted it needed to be done that day; they performed the procedure there and then, and I went back to work and said nothing. I was convinced it was because of the early abuse, so I sat in all my shame and guilt again.

I had to have smear tests every four months and routine examinations. During one of these examinations, my GP abused me. I froze; I was hot and sweating, panicking. I never told anyone about it. I was afraid that if I did, then it would come out about my past.

This was the final turning point for me, a realisation that I would remain a victim if I allowed myself to. While I had changed my circumstances, I hadn't addressed the beliefs and behaviors created by my past. I was still living with fear, shame, and guilt, terrified that my secrets would come to light and that I'd lose control of my life.

I was trapped in a relentless cycle of fear and exhaustion. Nightmares became a constant part of my sleep, dragging me back to the past no matter how much I tried to escape it. But staying awake wasn't any better; pushing the memories down during the day only made my anxiety worse at night. It became a vicious circle, one I couldn't break.

My heart would race for no reason, panic attacks would strike if I tried to be around family on social occasions, and I felt constantly on edge. My mind was scattered, unable to focus, unable to be present. I was stuck, caught between a past I couldn't change and a future I couldn't see. It felt like no matter how hard I tried to move forward, my trauma had a grip on me, refusing to let go.

But I wanted more for myself and Nathan. I realised that to create a better life for us both, I had to start with myself. I needed to confront my past and let go of the beliefs and behaviors that no longer helped me. I had lost touch with who I was, my soul, and my sense of self, and I knew I needed to rediscover myself.

I was no longer going to let my past define me. I had to take ownership of my healing and become the person I truly wanted to be. We are what we learn until we learn not to be.

The first thing I did was phone my mum and tell her that I needed to talk to her. Now, I couldn't back out. The next few days, the fear gripped me so tightly I could hardly breathe. My heart pounded, my hands trembled, and my mind raced with doubts. What if she didn't believe me? What if she blamed me? What if this shattered everything? I had carried this burden for so long, but speaking it out loud felt like stepping off a ledge into the unknown.

I waited until my stepdad was at work, as I needed her to be alone. Every second leading up to that conversation felt like an eternity, my chest tightening with each thought. Finally, I sat down, my voice barely above a whisper as I tried to explain how the past doesn't just stay in the past, how it lingers, shaping everything. Then, with every ounce of courage I could muster, I told her what my uncle had done to me.

I couldn't bring myself to go into detail. I couldn't tell her how long it had happened or the depths of my pain. I watched her face, shock, confusion, and disbelief. She insisted she had no idea, and I believed her. With everything she had been dealing with at the time, maybe she truly hadn't seen it.

But then, the moment I needed comfort the most, she said she didn't want to hear anymore. She didn't want to talk about it again. The weight I had carried for so long wasn't lifted; there was instead more silence, and the secrets remained. We never really spoke about it again. And when we finally did, much later, her words cut deeper than I ever thought possible. She wished I hadn't told her. She had to go to therapy because of what I had said. The weight of my truth, the pain I had lived with for years, became something she wished she could erase. At that moment, I realised I was still carrying it alone.

The second step was to get professional help. I would repeatedly make appointments at the doctor, intending to tell them about the abuse and ask for help, yet every time I found myself in the doctor's room, the words wouldn't come out. I had never said them out loud before, and I ended up making up some illness or excuse. One day, I asked the receptionist if I could speak to her privately, and she agreed, and we went into a quiet room. I told her I wanted help but could never get the words out. I told her I had been abused as a child, and she listened.

She said she would make an appointment for me and tell the doctor beforehand about our conversation so that they were prepared; there was no backing out now. I visited the doctor, told them my symptoms and about my past, and I was given anxiety medication.

My anxiety began to take more control of my life. I would look at Nathan, and the enormity of what had been done to me at his age started to hit home. How could someone do that to a child they were supposed to love? At my lowest point, I knew I couldn't do it alone.

Desperate for anything that might help me make sense of the turmoil inside, I turned to volunteer groups for support. Some offered group therapy, while others provided one-on-one guidance. Through them, I discovered that while external support was invaluable, true healing had to come from within.

As children, our experiences shape the core beliefs that guide us through life. But when those beliefs stem from trauma, they can keep us trapped. Healing meant confronting them head-on, listening to both my mind and body to understand my triggers. I came to see that these triggers no longer belonged in my present, and they had no place in the life I was working to build.

The next step was reclaiming my identity. I had spent so long defining myself by my trauma that I no longer knew who I was beyond it. I started small, visiting libraries and searching for books and guides that could help me understand myself better. I began keeping a "positive quality record," writing down moments of strength, kindness, and progress, the proof that I was more than my past. This simple habit helped me challenge the negative self-talk that had dictated my life for so long.

Trust had always felt dangerous, but I realised that if I wanted to build healthy relationships, especially with others and with myself, I had to let go of the fear that everyone would hurt me. Learning to trust again meant practicing self-compassion, being kind to myself, allowing mistakes, and forgiving myself for the things I wasn't responsible for.

Survival had been my focus for so long that I didn't know how to live. The coping mechanisms that once protected me,blocking out pain, shutting people out, and suppressing emotions were now holding me back. To move forward, I had to unlearn them and replace them with self-awareness, self-acceptance, and healing.

Healing wasn't about erasing the past, but about reclaiming my power over it. Every step forward, no matter how small, proved I was no longer trapped. A better life was waiting; I just had to keep going.

Acceptance became the key. It didn't mean condoning what had happened, but rather letting go of the resistance that kept me stuck. The sooner we face our experiences, the less power they have to control us.

That healing journey allowed me to rediscover joy and feel true gratitude for what I had. I was no longer just surviving, I was living. It cemented my strength, courage, and resilience, equipping me to face whatever challenges life might bring.

I was determined to create a life where I would no longer need to depend on people who could let me down. My son became my motivation, and I wanted to build a future he could be proud of.

I threw myself into my work, despite not having a strong academic background. I worked relentlessly, applying for promotions, volunteering for extra projects, and striving to prove myself. Each new challenge pushed me outside of my comfort zone, especially in the high-pressure, male-dominated world of manufacturing. But with every promotion and every success, my confidence grew.

I developed a strong reputation within the industry for delivering results and building trusted relationships, especially with large manufacturing clients like Ford and JLR. Eventually, I was headhunted by other companies who recognised the calibre of my work. For me, it wasn't just about career progression; it was about reclaiming control, creating stability, and building a life on my terms.

I met my soulmate, and together, we've built a beautiful life over twenty-six years of marriage. Between us, we have three wonderful children: my son, his son, and our daughter. My son and daughter achieved remarkable success in dance, competing and winning on stages around the world. Our daughter has also been on TV screens since she was eight and is now a successful businesswoman, while my son pursued his passion for music as a DJ and producer from the age of fifteen.

As a family, we've created unforgettable memories traveling to incredible places like Dubai, Mexico, the Dominican Republic, Ibiza, Palma, and Italy, where we visited the Ferrari factory and attended the F1. I cherish my close relationships with my children, particularly my daughter, with whom I often travel. We recently embraced the full clubbing experience in Ibiza, and I can honestly say I had the time of my life.

Beyond my achievements, I've made it a mission to help others. I've supported many children in finding their way to better lives and, in one of my proudest moments, became a live kidney donor to save my best friend.

Six years ago, we moved to a lovely village, a place filled with wonderful neighbours and new friendships. Life continues to bless me: my daughter has an amazing career, and my son is happily married with a child of his own while still pursuing his musical dreams.

I am living a life I could never have imagined. Don't get me wrong, we have faced some very challenging times. We suffered a stillbirth following a pregnancy filled with complications and covered up by the hospital, delaying the burial for three months. My daughter suffers from a life-threatening bleeding disorder that remains undiagnosed, and we were told she would probably not survive past sixteen. To try and control the disorder, she lost weight and later was diagnosed with anorexia and bulimia. We battled with health authorities to get the help she needed, which failed us at every level, resulting in two desperate suicide attempts.

I also endured an attempted rape by a stranger at knifepoint. It later transpired that he had raped several people, and he went to jail for the attacks.

I truly believe that without the work I did on myself early on in my life, I wouldn't have survived just one of these events, but with courage, strength, and resilience, I didn't just survive; I thrived, living the life I deserve.

**Affirmations & Final Words**

Thank you for taking the time to read my story. Through sharing my journey, I hope to inspire others who may be struggling with their own path to healing.

- You are not what happened to you,you are what you choose to become.
- Your past may shape you, but it doesn't define you; how you respond to it shapes your future.
- You deserve to live free from fear, shame, blame, and guilt.
- Your healing journey is valid, no matter how long it takes.
- It's okay to take back your power and control your own outcome.
- Live the life you deserve.

The quicker we accept and deal with what has happened in life, the easier it is to heal. No matter how small the issue or how shameful you feel, acknowledge it, accept it has happened, and let it go. Think of life's troubles as a glass of water, the longer you hold onto it, the heavier it becomes. Release your burdens sooner rather than later.

Remember that healing is a journey,a continual one. Strive for balance in all things. Don't let your goals get in the way of enjoying life; instead, let them enhance it. Take care of yourself from the inside out, eat well, exercise, and make time for joy.

Life will present challenges, but with the right tools and mindset, you can face them with courage, strength, and resilience. I found that the work I did on myself early in life equipped me to handle whatever came my way. You, too, can build this foundation.

If my story resonates with you, please know that you're not alone. Together, we can break the silence surrounding abuse and trauma. We can create a world where survivors don't just survive,they thrive.

For support on your healing journey or to connect with me:

*https://linktr.ee/andreabevansg*

## ABOUT THE AUTHOR

# ANDREA BEVAN

SCAN TO KNOW MORE

*Andrea's journey from Salford, Manchester, exemplifies the power of courage, strength, resilience and self-belief. Rising above childhood traumas with determination rather than degrees, she built an impressive career in manufacturing leading projects across Europe and America while helping countless others heal from trauma. As a mother, mentor, and live kidney donor, she demonstrates how adversity can be transformed into strength. Her story continues to inspire those seeking their own path to healing.*

CHAPTER

14

# Good As New

*Gaslit, Betrayed, Silenced*
*She Became the FireproofCEO™*

SHERRY DOUBLE

There were seasons of my life when silence felt like salvation. Not peace with a purpose—but the quiet that comes when chaos finally runs out of breath. I would have paid any price for it.

It sounds dramatic, but I'm not exaggerating. I wasn't chasing calm. I was desperate for the absence of pain. The absence of putting out fires that never stayed out.

I just wanted the storm to stop. Any storm. All of them, actually.

And there were many.

Some were quiet—the kind that smolder beneath the surface, slowly suffocating your joy. Others were loud, like the night I bled through my sheets and stumbled into the bathroom, shaking and terrified. Or the moment I held Remmy in my arms as she took her final breath—my anchor, my constant, suddenly silent.

Remmy was my shadow, my soft landing, the one who didn't care what I signed, closed, or brokered. She just loved. For seventeen years, she witnessed it all—the wins, the breakdowns, the traumas and the pivots I didn't speak aloud.

Her death was not a slow fade. Not a quiet passing in another room. But in my arms. One moment, warm. The next, gone.

It was an amputation without anesthetic. A silence so thick it screamed.

My body kept functioning, but something sacred had left with her last breath.

I couldn't explain it. I couldn't eat. I couldn't breathe.

Grief like that lives in your cells. It doesn't wail—it drowns. The kind that makes the world feel like it's still spinning, but you're no longer on it.

But the world didn't stop. It never does. The emails kept coming. My calendar didn't slow. Investors still wanted numbers and answers.

So I moved like a ghost in glam—heels, polished, smile fixed. My suit was perfectly tailored, but my soul was hemorrhaging beneath it.

There was no space to grieve at home either. That house had become a mausoleum of unspoken disappointment. No greeting. No warmth. Just a man who once adored me now barely lifting his eyes. Silence stacked on silence.

*Two years before the medical crisis*

Before fintech, my world was real estate. But not the glossy kind you see on TV. This was high-stakes, high-pressure, high-impact real estate. I wasn't just a broker. I was a dealmaker. Over the years, I negotiated and authored nearly a billion dollars in real estate transactions—seven- and eight-figure deals that shaped skylines, revived communities, and redefined possibility. I worked with developers around the globe, collaborating on large-scale projects, securing investment programs, and structuring deals that required grit, vision, and precision.

Outside the traditional property space, I raised capital through private equity and venture capital partnerships in everything from mining and waste-to-energy to net-zero construction, protein innovation, and even a boutique tequila company. Not every project was glamorous—but every one of them aimed at something better. Cleaner. Smarter. More sustainable. If it had the potential to improve lives, I found a way to back it.

I didn't just build deals. I built momentum. And I did it while holding space for complexity, for integrity, and for the belief that even in a world driven by numbers, purpose still matters.

At the time, my company felt like innovation. Gratitude gifting. Fintech with a heartbeat. But now I see it for what it really was: resurrection in disguise. It gave me something to build when everything else was burning.

And for a fleeting moment, it got his attention. For a breath, I thought he saw me again.

But it was never about the mission. It was about the mirror. If I succeeded, he absorbed the glow. If I failed, he recoiled.

My work wasn't mine. It was a reflection he judged himself by.

So I poured everything into the one place that felt like it was mine. I tried to rebuild myself through creation. Grandeur was his obsession. Purpose was mine.

But even purpose can't outrun pain. And my body had already begun its quiet rebellion.

What I didn't know then was that my body was trying to teach me the first principle of what would become my

Fireproof Framework: **Presence**. The art of listening to what your body is telling you, even when everyone else—including doctors—tells you you're wrong.

It started with whispers—subtle signs I dismissed. Bleeding. Fatigue. A mind fog I couldn't cut through. My head pulsed like a warning drum I kept silencing.

More coffee. More control. More pretending.

But my body—the one I had trained to perform and persevere—was trying to save me from myself.

I wasn't listening.

Until the night I woke up drenched in blood.

*Spring 2019*

Not metaphorically, but a harsh reality.

Sheets soaked. Hands trembling. Panic thick in the air. I stumbled to the bathroom and flipped on the light. And what I saw made my world tilt.

The bleeding was accelerating.

My heart thundered. This wasn't stress. This was something darker.

Still, I rationalized. I pushed through. Told myself there was no time for a breakdown.

My body was screaming. My mind kept sending red flags. A little voice kept whispering, "Get a second opinion." I had conversations with the doctor—more than once—but each time, I let her certainty override my own. That gnawing intuition—I ignored it. Again.

This was my first lesson in what I'd later call **Healing**—not just of the body, but of the relationship between self-trust and survival. Sometimes healing begins with refusing to be gaslit by your own fear.

After seven days in the hospital with a severe kidney infection—on painkillers strong enough to take down a tribe—they finally scheduled day surgery. I arrived at 6 AM, uneasy but compliant. By noon, I was discharged.

"You'll probably just need Tylenol," the doctor said.

She knew she had damaged me.

She had performed an ablation—burning the tissue to cauterize my uterus. But it wasn't just localized heat. She burned straight through, perforated my bowel, and then sent me home.

And as casually as one might toss out a compliment, she said it: "I sewed you up good as new."

She should have known there could have been more damage. Evidently, there was. But she didn't check. She didn't warn me. She simply dismissed me.

That was the first betrayal. The first negligence.

I wanted to believe her. I needed something to be easy. Despite the alarms sounding inside me, I clung to her certainty.

My mother, following the discharge instructions like gospel, walked me around the house every hour. The very thing she believed would help me—was quietly killing me.

Each step sent white-hot pain surging through my body. Still, I endured. Because I thought I was supposed to. Because I trusted the doctor.

But my body couldn't endure it.

*The same night*

The pain intensified by the hour. The fog rolled in. Sepsis was taking hold.

My strength vanished. By sundown, I collapsed.

It would take me two years to fully heal from what they missed in those five hours. Two years for my organs to recover.

That night, my friend came over. She saw what he didn't—that I was fading.

He said, "This is ridiculous, you need to go to bed."

Instead, she called an ambulance.

And that call saved my life.

I vaguely remember now the bright blur of traffic lights. The jolt of every pothole. The curses at every red light. Pain pulsed through every cell. Each brake sent a fresh wave of agony through my abdomen.

I faded in and out, unable to speak, hardly able to breathe. By the time we arrived, I was barely conscious.

They wheeled me into a quiet, dimly lit ICU—empty, sterile, and eerily silent. The isolation was suffocating. A chilling backdrop that felt less like care and more like concealment.

Something about the stillness made me feel erased, hidden away, as if my suffering were an inconvenience they needed to keep out of sight.

Their reassurances were smooth, clinical, and detached—offered with the same flat calm that had once dismissed my agony as Tylenol-manageable.

But the infection was real. The pain was real. The fear that wrapped around my chest and whispered that something was terribly wrong—that was real, too.

Here, in the ICU darkness, I learned **Ownership**. Not of blame, but of my own truth. I had to own what I knew in my bones, even when everyone else made me question it.

I was forced to fight not just for healing, but for truth. To believe what I felt deep within, even as they made me question it.

My gut—gnawing and insistent—kept telling me: this isn't over.

I didn't know it then, but I was stepping into the hardest fight of all—not just for survival, but for the belief that a comeback was still possible.

After the ICU, they moved me again. Not to a quiet recovery room, but to the labor ward—of all places. While new life was being brought into the world around me, I lay there invisible, fighting for my own. It wasn't healing—it was hiding. A surreal exile. One more way the system kept me out of sight, as if my suffering didn't belong.

Funny, looking back now—it was the perfect place for a rebirth. But at the time, I only felt erased.

A surreal backdrop of screaming mothers in the throes of childbirth played out around me, a jarring contrast to my own silent, internal battle. My screams were softer, yet each one was a cry for help that felt louder than the chaos around me.

They pumped me full of elephant doses of pain medication, but nothing could touch the tremors that wracked my body—convulsive shudders that threatened to tear me apart.

Eventually, my body gave in, collapsing into a merciful blackout.

That moment of relief was quickly shattered when the offending surgeon—the one who had broken me—shook me awake like I was an inconvenience, not a patient.

What followed felt scripted from a nightmare.

*Hour 6 of what should have been overnight observation*

They wheeled me down the hall, my body writhing in agony, and introduced me to what I can only describe as a surgical parade:

Two surgeons. Two anesthesiologists. A scrub nurse. A circulating nurse, on and on.

Each surgeon with their own entourage—the one who broke me, and the one brought in to save me.

No one had told my family I was being taken back in. The doctor had said I'd be admitted overnight, nothing more.

Thankfully, my friend had the instinct to tell my mother she'd stay with me. She had no idea what was about to unfold.

The betrayal cut deeper in that moment. It tore into tightly stitched layers of my past—where old wounds still smoldered. A secret I had carried alone for years, sealed behind silence, until the truth finally broke through and led to prosecution. That battle never truly ended. It lived inside me—buried, but breathing.

So when they lied to me, dismissed me, made me question what I knew in my bones—that old rage came roaring back. Their gaslighting didn't just deny my pain. It mirrored every betrayal I had survived. It pulled me back into the skin of my little girl who was taught to stay quiet, be small, and make others comfortable.

But I wasn't that girl anymore.

I wouldn't let them get away with it.

This is where **Empowerment** was born—not as a concept, but as a choice. The moment I decided I would never again make myself smaller to make others comfortable.

I became my own advocate—not by choice, but out of necessity.

The more they tried to silence me, the angrier I became. And the anger didn't weaken me—it sharpened me.

I questioned everything. I read between every line, every tone shift, every carefully chosen word. Alert to every form of subtle dismissal. I knew the playbook, and this time, I wasn't going to play along.

I stopped waiting to be saved and saved myself—believed myself.

Stopped trying to make myself smaller—I expanded.

They wheeled me down to the operating room, and just before taking me in, they presented me with a consent form, a document I couldn't even read in my drug-induced haze. A cosmic joke played on a broken body.

What choice did I have?

As I lay there, teetering on the edge of consciousness, a chilling thought pierced through the fog:

"If I go now, is this it? Is this how my story ends?"

And then, even softer but somehow louder: "How will I be remembered? Will I be remembered at all?" The question hollowed me out.

It wasn't just about dying—it was about disappearing. About being reduced to symptoms. Dismissed. Forgotten.

But somewhere inside me, something whispered back:

"No. Not like this."

And just like that—my eyes closed.

*Emergency surgery, Hour 1*

My body was a battlefield.

I learned later that they opened me up and lifted out my intestines—my actual guts laid on a tray. Contaminated. Inflamed. Compromised.

They washed what they could. Cut what they couldn't. My terminal ileum was removed. My insides resected and reconfigured in a last-ditch effort to save what was left.

I was one decision away from a colostomy bag. One misjudgment away from never fully coming back.

They dismantled me to salvage me.

When finally done, they closed me up with twenty-three staples and left behind titanium, permanently holding my bowels together. Cold. Unforgiving. Permanent.

The scar across my abdomen was not just physical. It was a punctuation mark on everything I had survived.

My family had been sent home, told I'd be admitted overnight for observation. Just silence across a six-hour window.

Beyond worried, they returned around 2:30 a.m., pacing the waiting room—searching for answers they didn't even know they needed.

When Dr. Death finally appeared—just before 7 a.m.—her flippant tone hadn't changed.

She poked her head into the room and said it again—those same three words that nearly cost me my life: "Good as new." That's the cruelty of gaslighting—when the lie is so casual, they don't remember repeating it.

But your body does.

My mother, a force of nature, was livid. But it wasn't just for the surgeon. In the hallway, she saw the nurse who had once rolled her eyes at my pain. The one who dismissed it as "princess complaints."

My mother squared her shoulders, looked her in the eye, and said:

"Guess she wasn't faking it after all."

I'm sure under her breath, she added: "Bitch."

*Recovery, Day 1*

When I finally woke up, I didn't feel whole. But I was alive.

Part woman. Part machine. A reconstructed version of myself, marked forever by what I had survived.

Funny how, as a girl watching *The Bionic Woman* reruns, I used to imagine myself as bionic—stronger, untouchable, superhuman. I just never thought it would look like this.

For twelve days, I lay tethered to machines—IV lines, oxygen, painkillers, anti-nausea drips, and iron infusions. I was no longer just recovering. I was recalibrating.

Eighteen pounds vanished. I became a shadow of myself. The mirror didn't show me—it reflected the cost. The fight. The wreckage.

But I was determined. I told myself I would get strong enough to leave.

And when I did—when they finally cleared me to go home—I went back to a house that still felt like an emotional void. The walls were the same. But something in me was not.

*Six weeks post-surgery*

Eventually, my days became a quiet rhythm—small sips, deep breaths, soft determination. And when I could, I made my way down the path to see my horses.

Rain. Truman. Blitz.

Each one had survived what should have broken them—former racehorses, now grounded warriors. Their injuries ended their careers but not their lives. Here, they healed at their own pace.

They didn't rush. They didn't ask for applause.

They just stood beside me. Quiet. Steady. Present.

They didn't care how strong I looked. They didn't ask for productivity. They mirrored the energy I was too raw to express: quiet survival.

They reminded me I had nothing to prove. That stillness was its own kind of power.

They gave me back the permission to return slowly. To not perform. To not explain. To just be.

With my horses, I learned **Intuition**—not as mystical knowing, but as the wisdom that comes when you finally stop performing and start listening.

I didn't know it then, but this stillness—this quiet, grounded presence—was the first flicker of something I wouldn't fully name until much later. A way of being that would eventually become the Fireproof Framework™.

But just as I was learning to move through that first flicker of healing, another betrayal arrived. This time, from my own skin.

*Eight weeks post-surgery*

Six weeks after I returned home, I noticed a pale patch on my right arm. Then another on my chest. Then my lower back.

At first, I thought it was just scarring. Some lingering wound from the trauma. But it spread.

When I showed my doctor, she brushed it off. "Impossible," she said. "Vitiligo doesn't just show up like that."

But my body wasn't interested in her certainty.

It was happening.

Vitiligo—an autoimmune disease where the body attacks its own pigment—it was bleaching pieces of me in slow motion.

My stitches were dissolving, but my skin was erasing me.

No one warned me. No one prepared me.

Each new patch felt like another disappearance. Another piece of me stripped away.

I wasn't ready for this version of me. I didn't know where it would stop—or if it would stop. My vanity, shaped by years of being on stage and in photos, couldn't comprehend what I was becoming.

Was this the price of survival?

Was I supposed to be grateful, even as I watched myself disappear?

So I turned inward again.

*Studio salvation*

I didn't know what I was looking for—only that I needed to find something that made me feel here. Not erased. Not abandoned by my body. Not invisible.

I picked up a pencil. Then a sketchpad. Then brushes. I didn't follow rules or techniques. I followed feeling.

I painted with urgency. With defiance. With the kind of abandon that doesn't ask for permission. I wasn't trying to be an artist. I was trying to breathe.

The studio became sacred.

While the man who once promised to care for me disappeared into his clinics, I disappeared into color.

YouTube became my art school. Acrylics my alchemy. I wasn't painting for praise. I was painting to survive.

Stroke by stroke, my confidence returned—not in polished form, but in raw expression.

Each canvas wasn't a product. It was a pulse.

And slowly, my identity returned. Not all at once. Not fully. But in fragments of color and movement. It reminded me that I could still create something new. Even if the old versions of me were gone.

In that studio, I discovered **Xpansion**—the truth that sometimes you have to lose yourself completely to find out who you really are.

But what I was rebuilding in that studio, he could not see.

And what I needed most—honesty, depth, intimacy—he could no longer give.

*Nearly twenty years together* and the distance between us stopped being emotional and became geographical. I left when the silence and disappointment became too much. When his embarrassment at my failures became too much. After nearly twenty years, that's when the fracture became final.

When I gathered my courage and strength, I moved into a beautiful waterfront condo. For the first time in a long time, I could breathe—without tiptoeing, without waiting for his critical tone. It was peaceful. Brief. But real.

Then, without warning, came the eviction—sudden and brutal.

Just when I thought I was finally reclaiming my breath, life yanked the rug out from under me. I had left a nineteen-year relationship—not casually, not easily, but with sadness and a spine forged from years of quiet suffering. I walked out with nothing but my will to live differently.

That condo wasn't just shelter—it was a symbol. A space where I could sleep without flinching, dance in the kitchen without judgment, and rediscover what it felt like to be safe in my own presence. For the first time in decades, I was learning to be mine.

And then—without reason, without mercy—I was told to leave.

No warning. No grace. Just one more collapse to navigate alone.

I packed my life into boxes that felt heavier than any suitcase should, not because of their weight, but because of what they represented: every inch I had clawed back, every shard of hope I had started to believe in.

I moved into storage. Holding my breath again. Putting parts of me back in metaphorical boxes. Wondering how much more I was supposed to endure.

Four months later, the entire storage facility was completely flooded. As if the universe wanted to test what was left of me.

Everything soaked. Everything gone. The last fragile threads of stability, washed away.

There I stood—soaked, stripped down, but standing. Grief still clung to me. But so did something else: Grit.

So I kept going. A thread of something stronger, a stubborn belief that better days were still ahead. Dad's voice: "Welcome to the first day of the rest of your life—now what?"

I had left behind the house, the horses, the history—not because I had to, but because I chose to. I refused to remain in a life I no longer believed in.

What you don't change, you are committed to. And I was done committing to what hurt me.

*The wildest thing I thought I would only dream of doing*

So I dug deep and did the wildest thing I thought I would only dream of doing.

Dubai—wasn't just a trip.

It was ignition. A declaration of self. A reclamation.

I would find her again—the version of me who once built empires.

From the moment I stepped off the plane, I felt it—something sacred in the air. Not just warmth on my skin, but possibility in my lungs.

I walked along the Marina at sunset, whispering promises to myself under my breath. The kind of promises you only make when you're finally ready to rise again.

The version of me who landed in that city was raw, stitched together with hope and borrowed courage. But each day, I gained a little more of myself back.

Sunsets were rituals.

I moved with presence.

I meditated. I lifted heavy things and let go of heavier ones—grief, resentment, the ache of what could have been.

I practiced healing. Not to erase what happened, but to make peace with it.

I made new promises. I made new friends. I reclaimed ownership of my time, my energy, and my worth.

I didn't just heal—I remembered.

I remembered what it felt like to want something more than survival. To feel empowered by joy, not burdened by it.

And in those moments, Fireproof stirred again. Quietly. Intentionally.

This wasn't the polished version of rebirth. It was messy, magical, elemental.

I wasn't chasing a comeback. I was reclaiming my fire.

And with that fire came vision.

I started to imagine what it might look like to bring others together—warriors like me, like us—who had been broken open and chose to rise anyway.

A space not for escape, but for return. A warrior's retreat.

Somewhere beautiful. Safe. Sacred.

Where presence was practiced. Where healing was held. Where ownership, intuition, and expansion weren't buzzwords—they were the air we breathed.

We wouldn't just rest there. We'd remember. Rebuild. Rise with ritual.

The very things that saved me—art, music, meditation—could be shared. Honored. Offered.

I wasn't just imagining a future. I was sketching the blueprint for something Fireproof.

*Two days before Dubai, the unimaginable call came in.*

"I'm still going," I announced. "I'm just changing my ticket."

Two days before my flight to Dubai, the unimaginable call came. "We think it's malignant; it's growing fast and changing shape." The doctor wanted me to cancel everything. Stay. Wait. Test. Follow up. But I had waited before—and it nearly killed me.

The Canadian healthcare system had failed me before. It was failing me again—but I wasn't finished yet.

My family, on that Mother's Day weekend, rallied around me after that shocking call. We spent the next several hours together, walking and talking. Each family member took turns cozying up to me with quiet reassurances, offering hugs, jokes, distractions—whatever I needed without needing to ask.

These are the six people I would trade my life for.

The next morning, I left the beach house with one goal: get the CT scan. The doctor had been clear—"5:30 AM. Only 3 walk-in appointments. Don't be late."

I didn't have the luxury of waiting. My medical records were read like a death wish—no doctor wanted to take me on. They didn't see a person, they saw paperwork. Risk. Liability.

But I refused to sit quietly. My body was screaming for justice.

Monday, 5:15 AM. I stood outside the clinic, a smile stretched across my face, masking the storm inside me. When the doors opened, I greeted the weary receptionist with energy I barely felt. She looked at me sideways and asked, "How are you so cheerful at this hour?"

I told her my story. Surface version only. Enough to let her see I wasn't there for routine care.

She shook her head, ready to turn me away, but then, from the back, a voice called out: "We take three walk-ins now."

*My angels,* I thought. *Watching. Moving the pieces.*

I got the scan. Out the door by ten to seven. Now... the wait.

Tuesday evening, true to my word, I boarded my flight to Dubai feeling liberated. Friends were concerned, some confused, about my decision to leave without clear results or a treatment plan. But I knew: waiting wasn't living. And something in me needed to breathe.

*Dubai, Week 1*

The scent of possibility was thick. Morning walks, visions of my retreat—spaces of warmth and grace. Sunsets, so spectacular they felt sacred. Meditation by the sea. Angel affirmations. Weightlifting. New friendships. Peace.

My mind, body, and soul lit up. I wasn't just happy—I was unapologetic. I was taking what felt like mine. Joy became my currency.

After returning from Dubai, I was scheduled to see an oncologist. Around the same time, I accompanied my mother to one of her appointments—and that's when the news landed like a hammer: her biopsy was malignant. Mine, still unknown.

We shared a look—two women, one younger, one shaped by decades of experience. My mother, the matriarch. Fierce. Wise. Steady. She met my eyes with a knowing that came from surviving. Beneath that knowing: the memory of her own mother, who had died from cancer years earlier.

But there was more behind that look. My mother grieved like clockwork. Every two years, a new goodbye: Her mother. Her nephew. Her father. Her brother. Loss after loss. Wave after wave.

And somehow—she still built a life that held love and laughter.

That's what survival looks like. Not avoidance. Not denial. But carrying grief like breath—present in every room, yet never stopping the living.

She didn't pretend. She didn't forget. She made room for joy anyway.

This is where I come from. This is what lives in me.

*When five doctors said no*

The next morning, she insisted my father go with me to the hospital for my own appointment. "You're not doing this alone," she said. Not a suggestion. A command.

We sat in the waiting room, my father and I—silent. Watching a teenage girl nearby, frail and clearly fighting for her life. I saw the strain on his face. His wife. His daughter. The same disease circling again. It aged him in real time.

Inside, I was spiraling. Not just from fear of another surgery, but from the weight of my mother's diagnosis and the trauma that still echoed in my body. I wasn't afraid of what they'd find—I was afraid of being handled again.

No oncologist would treat me without a confirmed biopsy. And no surgeon would perform the biopsy—not on me. Not with my history. I was problematic.

Paperwork—too complicated to touch.

Five doctors turned my file away. Seeking reprieve, I fled to Florida. My best friend, watching me unravel, suggested I meet with Dr. Q—a skilled plastic surgeon with experience in women's health and reconstruction.

We met casually. Just to strategize. Navigate the system.

But he looked up, steady and certain, and said, "Sherry, I can fix this."

It wasn't just the words. It was how he said them. No hesitation. No fear. He saw me—as a person. Not a risk.

And something in me softened. For the first time in years, I felt the tiniest edge of safety.

Then—miraculously—everything aligned. Finances. Schedule. The universe exhaled.

Seven weeks later, I was booked for surgery. And I just knew: it would be okay.

*The morning that changed everything*

The morning of my surgery, my best friend by my side—steady, quiet. Grounding me.

Outwardly, I was calm. Inside, I was a storm. The echoes of 2019 were still loud.

Hours later, I woke up in recovery—groggy, aching. I remembered Dr. Q's promise: no more staples. That mattered.

The pain was sharp. Constant. But I had known worse—and now I knew better.

Each day, I moved. Slowly at first—just standing. Then walking. I needed to reclaim my body. My power. My life.

Within a week, despite the pain, I insisted on dinner out. I needed to be in the world again. To feel like me.

Every step whispered: *You're coming back.*

The first weeks were brutal—full of discomfort, small failures, quiet wins. But I pressed on.

Three weeks after surgery, the call came—the results were in. I held my breath.

Dr. Q said the words I didn't dare hope for: **Benign.**

I called it "birthing an alien." Whatever it was, it had drained my life-force—and now it was out. It wasn't just tissue—it was every betrayal. Every time something was taken—my health, my home, my hope.

Birthing it wasn't just medical. It was spiritual. It was like birthing freedom.

Because when women rise, they don't just recover—they reinvent the world.

*—Sherry Double, Creator of the Fireproof Framework*™

Dr. Q played a role in saving me—not just physically, but by believing in my wholeness when others couldn't see it. But the truth is—I saved myself, too. I chose to keep going. I chose to trust my body, my instincts, and my worth. I hadn't just stitched back together. I had rebuilt myself—intentionally, fiercely, fully.

And I was ready—to rise. To share. To turn this story into light.

I hadn't just survived - I'd sculpted a blueprint from the ashes.

Because these fires weren't meant to consume me. They were meant to refine me.

Because **I AM FIREPROOF.**

I've carried it since I was a girl. It burned when I stood up at twenty-one and said no more. It burned through grief, through silence, through survival.

Now it has a shape.

A framework. A path. A way forward—not just for me, but for anyone who's ever wondered if they could come back from the unthinkable.

The Fireproof Framework wasn't born in theory. It was born in fire.

Not in a workshop. Not on a whiteboard.

But in the wreckage. In the darkness. In the long nights no one saw.

It emerged piece by piece—first as survival, then as awareness. Then as something I could share.

**Presence. Healing. Ownership. Empowerment. New Beginnings. Intuition. Expansion.**

Seven sacred steps. Seven human truths.

This framework became my compass—and now, my calling.

Even my miracle surgery—booked seven weeks after Dr. Q said he could fix me—proved the path works. I unknowingly followed it before I ever named it.

This isn't just healing. This is a powerful comeback. Because this? This is just the beginning.

Begin your own transformation. Let your fire speak.

If this chapter stirred something in you... I'd love to stay connected.

You can find me at @TheComebackWarrior or visit TheComebackWarrior.com to begin your own rise.

Let's rise—together.

## ABOUT THE AUTHOR

# SHERRY DOUBLE

SCAN TO KNOW MORE

*Sherry Double is a global entrepreneur, reinvention strategist, and bestselling author with 20+ years in real estate, finance, and cross-border investment across the UAE, US, UK, and Canada. After surviving childhood trauma, misdiagnosis, and medical betrayal, she turned her pain into power—and her power into purpose and profit. Sherry launched a brokerage, co-founded a fintech firm, and now leads a private investment circle. A champion for neurodivergent brilliance and trauma-informed leadership, she speaks worldwide on identity, resilience, and reinvention. Through the Fireproof Framework™, she helps high performers reclaim voice, rebuild legacy, and rise.*

# Transform Your Life at a LIVE EVENT

## Here's the ultimate gift for you:

As a token of gratitude, if you join the waitlist for the next book in the series and purchase that book too **you will receive a FREE ticket** to attend one of my **LIVE EVENTS** happening in cities around the world.

## Value Stacked Live Event - $1,000 value

Your past does NOT define you. Your COMEBACK does.

This is the event that will change everything.

Join Sir Marco Robinson and 10 guest speakers for a high-energy, no-BS, transformational event where you'll learn to turn your biggest challenges into your greatest success story—and build a high-impact, high-income personal brand.

This one-day transformational event is designed to inspire, empower, and equip you with tools to create the comeback story of your dreams.

You'll:

- **Meet me, Sir Marco Robinson, and some of the extraordinary authors** featured in this book series.
- **Hear exclusive live stories** of transformation, told directly from the authors themselves, that will ignite your belief in what's possible.

- **Gain revolutionary tools and strategies** to crush your goals, overcome setbacks, and rewrite your story with strength and purpose.
- **Network with like-minded warriors** who are also on their own comeback journeys—build connections that will fuel your growth.
- **Be part of a community that believes in you, your dreams, and your power to rise again.**

## PLUS: Bonus Gifts Worth $997 just for attending!

1. **Exclusive VIP Workbook** to guide you step-by-step as you implement what you've learn at the event.
2. Access to my **"How to Start Over" Digital Masterclass**, packed with insights, tools, and strategies to fuel your transformation journey.
3. A **One-on-One Virtual Coaching Session** with one of our featured authors, who will help you navigate your own personal comeback story.
4. Lifetime access to the **"START OVER" Community**, where you'll find ongoing inspiration, resources, and connections to keep you on track.

This event isn't just a ticket—it's an investment in the next, most extraordinary chapter of your life.

**To claim your free ticket**, Scan the QR code. Secure your spot now, as space is extremely limited at these events!

**Collect all 10 books in the series and attend a live event to be in with a chance of winning an incredible £100K Prize Fund to help you 'Start Over'!**

If you :

- Purchase all 10 books in the series (and send us proof of purchase) and
- Attend a live event (and upload a selfie of you with Marco along with the hashtag #SOwithmarco to instagram)
- Email admin@marcorobinson.com to let us know you want to pitch!
- And you'll be invited to send us a video to tell us about the idea you have for a transformational business you'd like to start to help others through the same challenge you've overcome.
- Marco will select his favourite 10 pitches and invite them to the second round!
- If selected you'll pitch to Marco in person and ONE lucky winner will win our incredible 100k 'Start Over' prize package!

Here's how it works :

Grand Prize: £50K cash + £50K mentoring (one winner)

Runner-Up Prizes:

- Two x **£10K cash grants** (two winners)
- **£1K rffle at every live event** (must be in the room to win).

## BE QUICK THOUGH! LIMITED SEATS ARE AVAILABLE AT EACH EVENT!

There are only 50 Free Seats Available at each live event so be quick and book yourself in as soon as you receive your free ticket. *You need to be in the room to be in with a chance of winning both the raffle for 1k AND to get your selfie for the Pitch!*

## Don't Miss the Podcast & VIP Newsletter

### Subscribe to the "HOW TO BE A HERO IN REAL LIFE" Podcast

Dive deeper into the "START OVER" journey with behind-the-scenes stories, actionable strategies, and interviews with the remarkable authors featured in this series. Every episode is designed to give you the tools and inspiration to rise above challenges and build a life you're proud of.

Scan the QR code

### Join the VIP Newsletter List

Be the first to hear about upcoming books, events, and exclusive offers. Plus, get access to bonus resources and transformational tips straight to your inbox. Subscribers are VIPs in the "START OVER" movement, receiving insights, updates, and tools to help you on your path.

# START OVER VOL 4

Scan the QR code

Your Comeback Starts Now

You've read the stories. You've seen the proof. Now, it's your turn. Don't let this book be the end—make it the beginning. Start your sensational comeback today by:

1. **Pre-ordering the next edition of "START OVER."**
2. **Claiming your FREE ticket** to one of my life-changing live events.
3. **Subscribing to the podcast and VIP newsletter** for ongoing support and tools.

Your journey is just beginning. The rest of your life is waiting for you to rise, rebuild, and **become the hero of your own story.**

With unwavering belief in your power to rise,
**Sir Marco Robinson**

Marco Robinson is an international #1 bestselling author, award-winning entrepreneur, and Top #2 Netflix producer. Renowned for creating and hosting Channel 4's prime-time TV show "Get a House for Free", where he gave homes to homeless families, Marco is a philanthropist knighted in the Commonwealth for his extraordinary charity work. A three-time winner of the prestigious Two Comma Club Award for generating millions in sales, Marco has built his legacy by inspiring people worldwide to turn loss into a sensational comeback. As the visionary behind the Start Over book series, he proves that no setback is too great to overcome.

Printed in Dunstable, United Kingdom

66425183R00188